SATISFIED

A 21-DAY PRAYER AND FASTING DEVOTIONAL THROUGH THE GOSPEL OF JOHN

Jeffrey Kent

CrossLink Publishing
RAPID CITY, SD

Kent/CrossLink Publishing
16012 Mt. Rushmore Road, Ste 3288
Rapid City, SD 57701
www.CrossLinkPublishing.com

Satisified / Jeffrey Kent. —1st ed.
ISBN 978-1-63357-393-2
Library of Congress Control Number: 2021934570

To my wife, Abigail, whose relentless faith and steadfast encouragement propel me to dream big and believe confidently in possibilities beyond what I can see.

Blessed are those who hunger and thirst for righteousness, for ***they shall be satisfied.***

Matthew 5:6

The backslider in heart will be filled with his own ways,but a good man will be ***satisfied from above.***

Proverbs 14:14 NKJV

I am the bread of life. Your fathers ate the manna in the wilderness, and they died. This is the bread that comes down from heaven, so that one may eat of it and not die. I am the living bread that came down from heaven. ***If anyone eats of this bread, he will live forever.*** *And the bread that I will give for the life of the world is my flesh.*

John 6:48–51

Contents

INTRODUCTION

Each year my church, as so many churches across the nation do, goes through a 21-day fast at the beginning of the year. Over the past decade, I have gone through an array of different types of fasts, prayer plans, and Bible reading schedules over the three-week period. Some have gone really well and some, I must admit, I failed at pretty early on!

There are a number of great resources to help in choosing and preparing for a fast, a few are highlighted in the first chapter of this book. However, the purpose of this devotional is not centered on fasting but in growing spiritually during a fast.

Sadly, I have seen so many people, including myself, put a tremendous amount of preparation into beginning a fast—buying the right foods, choosing some recipes, setting daily meal plans—but yet they neglect the spiritual aspect of the fast. The 21-day fast becomes a three-week diet plan and we feel no closer to God and no more matured spiritually than when we began. We are denying physically but not filling spiritually.

In any spiritual fast, what we will put down is certainly important, but what we will pick up is far more important. As we deny our flesh, we must then begin to allow God to fill our spirits. If not, what we experience is simply emptiness. We trudge through the three weeks, fighting hunger pangs, headaches, possibly withdrawals from social media. By the end, we've forgotten why we did it in the first place, perhaps just so we can say we did—another Christian merit badge to add to our collection

I often get asked by people wanting to grow spiritually but struggling where to start. The common question is, "Where do I begin?" It is easy to begin to feel overwhelmed. "I want to start reading the Bible, I want to build up my prayer life, I want to learn how to fast, but where do I start?"

Satisfied is a 21-day devotional to help you on that journey. Regardless of where you are in your spiritual walk, I believe that during these next three weeks can be pivotal in growing more intimate in your relationship with God and finding freedom in areas of your life as you learn to deny yourself, push into God, and watch him empower you through his Spirit!

When people who are new to their faith or have never really studied the Bible ask me how to begin reading God's Word, I always like to suggest beginning in the Gospels. If God's Word is all about Jesus, then begin with Jesus! Each of the four Gospels—Matthew, Mark, Luke, and John—are distinct and reveal different aspects of the person of Christ, but John is perhaps my favorite to begin with. It is often called the "spiritual gospel." It is unique in its symbolism and in telling us who Jesus really was—the Word of God, the Light of the World, the Bread of Life, the I AM.

Satisfied will take you through the entire Gospel of John, one chapter a day. Each day has a key theme for you to focus on throughout the day as you allow God to reveal himself to you in new ways. You will also have one other key chapter from the Bible to support the theme. This will give you two chapters a day to examine, to reflect on, to apply to your life, and lastly, to pray as God reveals truths to you based on the theme of the day.

This devotional takes some commitment. It may stretch you in ways that you have not as you take the plunge to soak up more of God—through his Word, through prayer, through meditation, and through fasting. Another essential aspect of this journey will be committing to quieting the distractions around you to hear the Holy Spirit as he speaks to you.

With two chapters a day and a reflection, one suggestion would be to go through one for each meal of the day. You can then finish the day out with praying over what God has spoken to you! If this is your first time studying God's Word and the amount of material or the time commitment is intimidating to you, you may want to spread each day out across an entire week. Instead of a 21-day study, you can turn it into a 21-week study.

The themes and chapters in this devotional were specifically chosen because they are some of the most central to the Christian faith. My prayer for you is that by the end of this you will have a greater understanding of the Gospel and the person of Jesus. I pray that God will open up within you an even greater desire to study his Word and to know more of him. I pray that through the living water and living bread that Christ offers, you will be satisfied!

The grass withers, the flower fades,
but the word of our God will stand
forever.

Isaiah 40:8

CHOOSING THE RIGHT FAST

Fasting without mercy is worthless to him who fasts. Let us fast, humbling our souls as the day draws near on which the Teacher of humility humbled himself becoming obedient even to death on a cross.

Saint Augustine

WHY FAST

Before launching into your 21 days, it's important to spend time in prayer and choose the right fast. But even more important than that is answering for yourself one foundational question: Why should I fast?

In a society where self-indulgence rules the day, little can be found promoting self-control or, even more, self-denial. Advertisements flood our eyes and ears through various forms of media fighting to convince us of what we need—more comfort, more luxury, more satisfaction—better health, better taste, better experience.

Yet standing in stark contrast to this barrage of self-worship is the Word of God. For those who wish to follow Jesus, he first calls them to deny themselves (Matthew 16:24; Mark 8:34; Luke 9:23, 14:26). Although the practice has sadly been greatly neglected in the church today, the Bible mentions fasting specifically some seventy-seven times.

Fasting is most often linked to prayer. Why is this? Because as people denied themselves physically, they pressed into all the more spiritually. You have perhaps heard it said that those who experience blindness often notice their other senses begin to heighten. In the same way, as we choose to silence some of our fleshly impulses, our spiritual senses can similarly heighten. However, fasting that lacks a spiritual drive and is not bathed in prayer is little more than a diet.

Fasting was an understood basic spiritual discipline for Jesus's followers. He said, "When you fast..." The keyword was not *if* but *when.* Fasting should be part of the normal Christian experience in the same way prayer and worship are. Biblical fasting is also often done with a purpose in mind, possibly to better hear from God, while in communion with God, while fighting temptation, in response to repenting from sin, when needing to make a major decision, or in preparation for a season of ministry.

Fasting can radically reset your priorities. It can fine-tune your spiritual antennas and allow the Holy Spirit to speak to you in clearer and richer ways. Through fasting, God can deepen your prayer, your Bible reading, and our worship experiences. Fasting can uncover spiritual blind spots that you have been neglecting. If you are seeking direction for a major decision in your life or help in overcoming a temptation, fasting can allow God to show you his will and empower you to walk in it.

Consider the young, Jewish prophet Daniel. In a foreign land and facing incredible temptation to abandon his beliefs and cave in to pressures to go against his beliefs, he decides to refuse the king's food and wine for 21 days. As he finished the fast, he received a revelation from God. A figure appeared to him in a vision and spoke to him the words of the Lord. The figure said that he heard Daniel's prayers as he humbled himself, prayed, and cried out to God.

> *In those days I, Daniel, was mourning for three weeks. I ate no delicacies, no meat or wine entered my mouth, nor did I anoint myself at*

all, for the full three weeks. On the twenty-fourth day of the first month, as I was standing on the bank of the great river (that is, the Tigris).

I lifted up my eyes and looked, and behold, a man clothed in linen, with a belt of fine gold from Uphaz around his waist ... Then he said to me, "Fear not, Daniel, for from the first day that you set your heart to understand and humbled yourself before your God, your words have been heard, and I have come because of your words.

Daniel 10: 2–5, 12

WHAT TO FAST

As you pray for God to reveal the right fast for you for these 21 days, there are two things to keep in mind.

1. If you feel led to choose a fast that would be a major change or disruption to your normal eating habits, and especially if you have any underlying health issues or are on medication, you should first consult your doctor before beginning your fast.

2. Fasting involves sacrifice. God honors our sacrifice. The choice is only between you and God, but as you choose a fast, choose something that will actually mean something to you.

Here are six of the more common fasts people may choose during a period of individual or corporate fasting. Often a food fast will be paired with a non-traditional fast as well.

1. **Traditional or Full Fast**—Liquids only. This may be water only or water, juices, and broths.
2. **Absolute Fast**—No food or liquid. Again, this should only be done after consulting a doctor.
3. **Daniel Fast**—No meats, breads, sweeteners, or processed food. This fast has become quite popular recently. There are plenty of Daniel Fast guides and recipes.
4. **Intermittent Fast**—Abstaining from food for certain hours throughout the day. This has become popular for health purposes. It may include fasting one or two meals a day.
5. **Sexual Fast**—Abstaining from sexual fulfillment to better devote yourself to prayer (1 Corinthians 7:5).

6. **Non-Traditional Fast**—This can include anything that has a strong influence or control over you physically, such as TV, cell phone, entertainment, social media, coffee, or fast food.

GREAT RESOURCES ON FASTING

Celebration of Discipline: The Path to Spiritual Growth (chapter 4) by Richard Foster

Fasting: Opening the Door to a Deeper, More Intimate, More Powerful Relationship with God by Jentezen Franklin

Fasting for Breakthrough and Deliverance by John Eckhardt

Spiritual Disciplines for the Christian Life (chapter 9) by Donald Whitney

DAY 1

The Word of Life

John 1 - Luke 2

In the beginning was the Word, and the Word was with God, and ***the Word was God****. He was in the beginning with God. All things were made through him, and without him was not any thing made that was made.* ***In him was life****, and the life was the light of men. The light shines in the darkness, and the darkness has not overcome it ... And the Word became flesh and dwelt among us, and we have seen his glory, glory as of the only Son from the Father, full of grace and truth.*

John 1:1–5, 14

Congratulations on beginning your 21-day journey! You'll be diving into two chapters a day, reflection, application, and prayer; o, be sure you have a schedule worked out so that you are prepared to not only succeed at this but also to hear from God! You have chosen to give something up in your life in order to gain something much more important which is God's Spirit, his Word, and a deeper relationship with him. Jesus chose you and gave up something for all of us as well, his life on this earth.

Today may be hard because your mind and body will begin to push back as you change up your usual routine. Jesus upset the normal routine of those around him as well, from the usual religious customs to the ones that left everything they had to follow him. It was a hard journey to complete to the end, and in the last few days, feeling all alone he asked that the cup pass from him. Knowing that he would finish, he became victorious. You can gain victory as well in this challenge. Commit now to not let your body win! Now let's journey to find satisfaction through the richness of God's Word and find a renewed thirst for his righteousness.

EXAMINING THE WORD

Read John 1
In the beginning was the Word. Think about the Word of God. How does John describe the Word in verses 4–5?

In verse 14, John says that we have now seen the glory of God through Jesus, his Son. His glory is full of grace and truth. Describe what each of these words means to you.

Grace:

Truth:

John the Baptist refers to Jesus in verse 29 as the "Lamb of God." Why do you think he would use this title?

Read Luke 2
Shepherds were watching over flocks of sheep. Why do you think God chose them to be the first to witness and declare the birth of Christ?

Write out what the multitude of heavenly hosts proclaimed in verse 14.

Simeon uses two words to describe the newborn Savior—***salvation*** (verse 30) and ***light*** (verse 32). What does each of these words describing Jesus mean to you? (For salvation, also look at Matthew 1:21; for light, look again at John 1:5.)

Salvation:

Light:

The prophetess Anna worshipped with fasting and prayed in the temple day and night. As Jesus was blessed by Simeon in the temple, she began to give thanks to God and speak to all who were waiting for the redemption of Jerusalem. Today begins the first day of your 21-days of fasting. What do you think kept her going to faithfully continue fasting day and night?

REFLECTING ON THE WORD

The theme for today is **the Word of Life**. In the opening chapter of John's Gospel, he describes Jesus as the "Word of God." The Greek term translated into English as *word* here is *logos*. *Logos* carries a lot more weight than the English translation *word* does. The *logos* of God describes the mind of God, the thought of God—the very nature of God. In these few opening verses of John, what do we learn about the nature of Jesus as the Word of God?

- Jesus is ***ETERNAL***. He was there at the beginning of creation. John makes it clear; he wasn't just with God at the beginning, but he is God.
- Jesus is the ***CREATOR***. At creation, as God spoke out over the great expanse, the Word went out and brought it to life. Nothing more was needed in the act of creation in Genesis 1 than simply the Word of God.
- Jesus brings ***LIFE***. All life has come through his life-giving power. John adds a repetition of this in verse 3 by stating the positive—all things were made through him, and then the negative of the same truth—and without him was not anything made that was made. He is reinforcing the idea to leave no

room for doubt that all life comes through the source of life: Jesus.

- Jesus is ***LIGHT***. He shines through the darkness, and the darkness is powerless before him. As Simeon held him, he saw the salvation power within him. He declared Jesus as the light that brings revelation to the Gentiles and the glory of God to Israel.

John the Baptist sees Jesus coming toward him and cries out, "Behold, the Lamb of God, who takes away the sin of the world!" Think about how right after the Gospel describes Jesus as the Word of God, it immediately declares him also as the Lamb of God. From all-powerful God to feeble lamb, from creator to creation, from giver of life to bearer of the sin of all mankind. To know this paradox is to know Christ and the heart of God for you and me.

The people of Israel depended upon sacrificial lambs, spotless and without blemish, for centuries as they tried to make atonement for sin. Though endless lambs were sacrificed, not one of these was a perfect offering. None of these was eternal. None of these had the power to truly overcome sin and death.

But there is good news! Jesus was the perfect offering. Through his sacrifice, he has reconciled us to the Father.

Jesus is the Word of God. His sacrifice was sufficient because within him is the very power of God. He is eternal; he is the source of all life; he is the light of the world. Though he is all those things, he also freely laid his life down. There is no better way to begin this fast than to recognize who Jesus truly is and the sacrifice he paid for you and me.

APPLYING THE WORD

What is something you are hoping to gain from this 21-day journey? Is there anything that makes you feel nervous or intimidated?

Jesus is the eternal Word of God, but his heart is for you! What does it mean to you knowing that you are the crown of his creation, that he stepped down from heaven just to set you free?

Jesus is the bringer of all life. Wherever you are in life, whatever situation you are facing, he can bring life. What are some areas you need Jesus to bring life to?

Jesus is the true light. He brings light into darkness. He also gives that light for you to be a light to others. What are areas in your life—family, work, friends, mind, emotions—that need the light of Jesus now? How can God use you as a light for others this week?

PRAYING THE WORD

In the space below, write out something that especially stood out to you from today's Bible reading. It may be a verse you read, something from the devotion, or just a thought that God gave you. As you close out today's devotion in prayer, pray this back to God as a commitment to him.

DAY 2

Cleanse the House

John 2 - Colossians 3

If then you have been raised with Christ, ***seek the things that are above****, where Christ is, seated at the right hand of God. Set your minds on things that are above, not on things that are on earth. For you have died, and your life is hidden with Christ in God. When Christ who is your life appears, then you also will appear with him in glory.* ***Put to death therefore what is earthly in you****: sexual immorality, impurity, passion, evil desire, and covetousness, which is idolatry.*

Colossians 3:1–3

Why 21 days? In the Old Testament, the prophet Daniel fasted from King Nebuchadnezzar's food and drink for 21 days. After only ten days of fasting, the Bible tells us that they looked stronger and healthier than all those who continued to eat the royal food (Daniel 1:15–16). It wasn't just about a health plan though. Daniel humbled himself before the Lord. He put his own life in danger by standing up for his faith. At the end of the fast, he received a prophetic vision from the Lord for God's people.

The theme for today is **cleanse the house**. After one day of denying yourself in this fast and setting a schedule to stay consistent with the reading, you may have already recognized some areas in your life that you need to clean house. Pay attention to the parts of your flesh that are fighting against you, that are crying out to be gratified. As you begin to overcome your physical desires, the desires of your soul can begin to be heard.

EXAMINING THE WORD

Read John 2

Jesus's very first miracle was transforming the water into wine at Cana. John writes in verse 11 that in doing this, Jesus manifested or revealed his glory. What does that mean to you?

Jesus said to those selling pigeons, "Do not make my Father's house a house of trade." Write out what his disciples remembered in verse 17.

Pay close attention to verses 23–25. The crowd believed Jesus only because they saw what?

Jesus, who is all-knowing, did not entrust himself to them because he knew what was in their hearts. Why do you think Jesus felt this way about those who believed in him only because of signs and wonders?

Read Colossians 3

Paul encourages us to put to death certain things in verses 5 and 8 and then in verse 12 he tells us to put on certain things. Write out the things we need to take off and put on. Which ones speak to you personally?

Write out verse 17.

REFLECTING ON THE WORD

Each passage today shows the distinct difference between those who are true followers of Christ and those who are not. There is debate as to whether the cleansing of the temple that takes place in John 2 is the same event recorded in the other Gospels (Matthew 21; Mark 11; Luke 19) or a different cleansing at the outset of his public ministry. Whether there were one or two cleansings of the temple, ask yourself, "What is Jesus trying to reveal to us about the heart of God in this?"

Consider this—Jesus went up to the Temple Mount in Jerusalem and drove out those making a mockery of the temple and extorting from the people of God. It would seem that he was trying to protect this physical place from being defiled, right? Yet only days later the veil to the temple would be torn in two, and the Spirit would come to fill the hearts of the believers. Even the practice of animal sacrifice would come to an end in Jerusalem less than forty years later. Even the temple itself would be destroyed in a few decades.

If it all was coming to an end, why is Jesus so passionate about cleansing this space? As John wrote in verse 17, remembering the prophecy of Psalm 69:9, "Zeal for your house will consume me." What was his house? John also wrote, "He was speaking about the temple of his body." The New Testament writers later saw that the church became the living temple of God.

> *Do you not know that you are God's temple and that God's Spirit dwells in you?*
>
> **1 Corinthians 3:16**

> *You yourselves like living stones are being built up as a spiritual house, to be a holy priesthood, to offer spiritual sacrifices acceptable to God through Jesus Christ.*
>
> **1 Peter 2:5**

If we are now the temple, this means we are now the dwelling place of the Spirit of God. He has chosen to use us to show his glory across the world. He has chosen us, his church, to be a light in the darkness and to testify of his goodness.

With the Spirit of God living within us, Paul urges the church to "Set your minds on things that are above, not on things that are on earth" (Colossians 3:2). He tells the church, the living temple of God, to again cleanse the temple! Put to death the things that don't belong in the church and above all things, put on love. Jesus did not cleanse out of anger. He did not drive out the wicked out of hatred. He did it out of love. A zeal for his house consumed him!

What does a church look like that is filled with the Spirit and daily putting on the love of Christ? Look at Colossians 3:15–17. It is filled with the peace of Christ. It is thankful. The Word of Christ is evident in teaching and worship. In ***ALL*** that the church does, they are doing it "*in the name of the Lord Jesus, giving thanks to God the Father through him.*"

APPLYING THE WORD

Jesus said a zeal for his house consumes him. That is why he was so passionate about cleansing it.

Has this fast brought to light anything in your life that may need to be cleansed?

Why do you think it is so hard for us to believe what we can't see?

Paul says in Colossians 3:14 that above everything else, we must put on love. In the same way, we begin our days by putting on clothes, how can you start your morning off with putting on love?

PRAYING THE WORD

In the space below, write out something that especially stood out to you from today's Bible reading. It may be a verse you read, something from the devotion, or just a thought that God gave you. As you close out today's devotion in prayer, pray this back to God as a commitment to him.

DAY 3

Love That Never Fails

John 3 - Romans 8

And we know that for ***those who love God all things work together for good****, for those who are called according to his purpose... No, in all these things we are more than conquerors through him who loved us. For I am sure that neither death nor life, nor angels nor rulers, nor things present nor things to come, nor powers, nor height nor depth, nor anything else in all creation, will be able to separate us from* ***the love of God*** *in Christ Jesus our Lord.*

Romans 8:28, 37–39

In a physical fast, Day 3 is usually the hardest. Whether you're doing a traditional fast, Daniel fast, or maybe just no caffeine, this is usually when your flesh starts fighting back. You may be experiencing hunger pangs or headaches. It seems inevitable that as soon as you start a fast, everyone wants to invite you to dinner! Everyone at work wants to bring their favorite dessert!

A fast is not just about denying yourself. It's about replacing the physical with the spiritual. As you hunger, remember that it's for a purpose. Let the cravings drive you to crave more of God and his Word. What better topic for today than love? There is no better motivator than to love and know that you are loved.

EXAMINING THE WORD

Read John 3

Jesus met with Nicodemus, a Pharisee, late in the evening. Why do you think he would want to meet with Jesus at night?

Why do you think John 3:16 is often considered the most famous verse of all in the Bible?

Write out John 3:16–17 in your own words. Personalize it by using "me" or your name in the place of "world."

Jesus says he is the bridegroom and we are the bride. Who does he say has eternal life in verse 36?

Read Romans 8

Read Romans 8:1 several times. Summarize it in your own words.

When our own words fail us in crying out to God, think about what verse 26 tells us the Spirit does for us.

Look at verses 35–39, what can separate you from God's love?

REFLECTING ON THE WORD

The two chapters today focused on the love of God. Each of them shows us a **love that never fails**. They remind us that in the midst of our chaotic lives, in the middle of a world seemingly filled with pain, selfishness, pride, hatred, anxiety, depression, and death, there is a better way. There is a higher plane.

If the Spirit of God lives within us, we are fully set free from all of the sin and darkness of this world and we are invited to walk in the love of God. What do we know about the kind of love that God offers to us from these chapters?

- **God's love for you and me is so great that Jesus came.** He stepped out of divinity and into humility. He willingly faced rejection and suffering to the point of death on the cross so that the very bondage of sin and death itself would be defeated.

- **True love does not bring condemnation.** Jesus did not come to condemn but to provide a way to salvation.
- **The greatest of all gifts, qualities, or attitudes is love.** Spiritual gifts are important, faith is essential, but without love, they lose their authenticity.

> *So we have come to know and to believe the love that God has for us. God is love, and whoever abides in love abides in God, and God abides in him.*
>
> **1 John 4:16**

- **Love matures us spiritually.** Love teaches us to put away childish ways and to walk as people who know God and are known by God.
- **Love never fails.** For those of us who are in Christ, nothing can separate us from his love. We are not called to just survive, to just get by. In Christ, we are more than conquerors! In Christ, we have confidence that nothing—no height, no depth, or anything else in all creation—can separate us from the love that God has for us and that he reconciled through the sacrificial work of Jesus.

How freeing is it to know that the love God has for us is not based on our performance. Neither our accomplishments nor our failures impact the level of love God has for us. Why is that? Because it is sealed in the perfect work of Christ.

You are not loved because of what you do but because of what he did. If you are in Christ, then his love is in you. It is an eternal, unbreakable love. In his love, we can be vulnerable. We can begin to break down walls. In his love, we also begin to discover our spiritual gifts and what it means to walk in the Spirit.

APPLYING THE WORD

How would you define love?

Consider the fact that God loved us so much that he gave his only Son. Jesus laid down everything and came to endure suffering and death, all for one reason—you and me. What does this kind of love mean to you?

Look at how Paul describes love in 1 Corinthians 13:4–7. Which attributes do you feel you are strong in?

Which attributes do you need God to mature you in?

Read Romans 8:1. What are some things that have caused you to feel condemnation? What are some things that have caused you to feel free in your relationship with Jesus?

PRAYING THE WORD

In the space below, write out something that especially stood out to you from today's Bible reading. It may be a verse you read, something from the devotion, or just a thought that God gave you. As you close out today's devotion in prayer, pray this back to God as a commitment to him.

DAY 4

Thirsting for Living Water

John 4 - Luke 15

Jesus said to her, "Everyone who drinks of this water will be thirsty again, but whoever drinks of the water that I will give him will ***never be thirsty again****. The water that I will give him will become in him a spring of water welling up to eternal life."*

John 4:13–14

Today we are discussing thirsting. You will read about a woman who went to draw water and then was introduced to a living water—a water that would quench her deepest needs. Let today's passage speak to you today. Let it speak directly to what you are hungering and thirsting. Jesus said in Matthew 5:6 that those who hunger and thirst for righteousness will be **satisfied**.

As you go through the two chapters in Examining the Word each day, you may struggle with some of the questions. Remember that this is your time of devotion with God. Many questions are not about finding the "right" answer but challenging yourself to truly think about what Scripture is saying and maybe to begin to see some passages in a different light.

EXAMINING THE WORD

Read John 4

When Jesus met the Samaritan woman, his first words to her were, "Give me a drink." The woman refused his request. When Jesus then began to reveal to her the living water that he could give her that would give her eternal life, how did she respond?

Write out verses 23–24.

In verse 35, Jesus tells his disciples to look up and see. What do you think Jesus and the disciples were seeing? Compare this to verse 30.

What happened in Samaria as a result of the woman's testimony?

Read Luke 15

Think about each of the three lost items. Who lost them, and what did they do when what was lost was finally found?

1. Parable of the Lost Sheep

   Who lost it?

   What did he do when it was found?

2. Parable of the Lost Coin

   Who lost it?

   What did she do when it was found?

3. Parable of the Prodigal Son

   Who lost him?

   What did he do when he returned?

REFLECTING ON THE WORD

Our theme for today is **thirsting for living water**. In the middle of the heat of the day, Jesus came to Jacob's well in Samaria. Wearied from his hurried travel to distance himself from the Pharisees—as his time had not yet come to pay the ultimate sacrifice—he sat as the disciples went to find food.

A woman approached the well under the midday sun. The fact that she was a woman, a Samaritan, and was of questionable moral character were three no small reasons for any upstanding Jew to have avoided her. And yet, Jesus made a simple, yet bold, request. He petitioned the woman to draw him some water from the well.

As we reflect on today's theme of thirsting for living water, recognize that it was not her thirst that brought her to Jesus. It was Jesus's thirst that brought him to her. He thirsted for water after a long trip, but more than that, he thirsted for the soul of a woman who had lost who she was. She saw in herself a lifetime of bad decisions and failed relationships. Jesus saw her true identity—the very first person to share the Good News of Jesus to the nation of Samaria.

She laid down the fear that led her to go draw water in the middle of the day and through the power of Christ, she ran into town proclaiming the Messiah. Jesus used this opportunity as the townspeople were coming to show his disciples that the fields are ripe. People are thirsty for the love of God. He's just looking for people who will go.

In the parables of the lost things in Luke 15, Jesus uses these allegories to demonstrate a profound truth about the heart of the Father. It is not our thirst for him that draws him to us, but it is his unquenchable thirst for us that leads him to seek us out—to restore us—to heal us—to bring us home.

In each of the three parables, those who found what was lost rejoiced. They represented the Father stopping at nothing to bring home one lost and broken child. And when that happens, all of heaven rejoices! The angels break out into celebration! Our Father in heaven prepares a feast like no other. He robes us in His righteousness. He restores us to our rightful place as heirs of God. He prepares a great banquet in which all of heaven can rejoice.

APPLYING THE WORD

How is your fast going? Is it causing you to thirst for anything new?

The woman at the well thought that she was only there to tend to her physical thirst, but Jesus showed her that she had spiritual thirsts—for intimacy, for companionship, for love, for acceptance—that she had been trying to fill in all the wrong places. He introduced her to living water. What are some needs you have had in your life that you've tried to fill in places apart from what Jesus can provide?

Are there any hidden matters of your heart—unforgiveness, anger, lust, hatred—that you need to give to Jesus and allow him to set you free from?

Thinking about the parable of the prodigal son, do you see yourself as the son who needs to come home to the love and acceptance of the Father or the son who is more wrapped up in performance and religion than compassion? As the younger son, see God running for you to embrace and restore you. As the older son, see God gently coming to show you his heart and to remind you that all that he has is you (Luke 5:31).

PRAYING THE WORD

In the space below, write out something that especially stood out to you from today's Bible reading. It may be a verse you read, something from the devotion, or just a thought that God gave you. As you close out today's devotion in prayer, pray this back to God as a commitment to him.

DAY 5

Stay Alert

John 5 - Mark 13

But concerning that day or that hour, no one knows, not even the angels in heaven, nor the Son, but only the Father. ***Be on guard, keep awake.*** *For you do not know when the time will come ... And what I say to you I say to all:* ***Stay awake.***

Mark 13:32–33, 37

Today I want to encourage you in your fast—don't give up! You may be experiencing some discouragement. You may feel overwhelmed, like this journey is all too much for you. Today you will read about a man who was stuck waiting for healing, something to happen in his life, for thirty-eight years. Be patient. Even when you can't see it, God is building you up and preparing you for greater things.

> *Seek the Lord and his strength; seek his presence continually!*
>
> **1 Chronicles 16:11**

EXAMINING THE WORD

Read John 5

Jesus met a man who had been an invalid for thirty-eight years and asked him, "*Do you want to be healed?*" Surely that was the only reason he was there at the healing waters. Why do you think Jesus asked him that question in verse 6? Look also at Mark 10:51.

Jesus had to stay alert. Religious leaders were daily trying to catch him in breaking a commandment. How did Jesus respond to his persecutors in verse 17?

Jesus said in verse 24 that whoever does what two things has eternal life?

Look at verse 39. When we read the Bible, how should we read it? What should we search for in all Scripture?

Read Mark 13

In discussing the signs of the end of the age, Jesus tells his disciples that they will face great persecution. What is the purpose (verse 10) and what is the promise (verse 11)?

Purpose:

Promise:

In verse 26, Jesus said that we will see the Son of Man come again in great power and glory. Though he tells them we will not know when, he does give them one command—stay alert. Summarize verses 32–37.

REFLECTING ON THE WORD

One of the beautiful things about the man who was healed at the pool of Bethesda is the innocence and simplicity of his faith. Jesus knew he wanted to be healed, but as he often did, Jesus made the man say what he needed. There is power in confession.

> *When the righteous cry for help, the Lord hears and delivers them out of all their troubles.*
>
> **Psalm 34:17**

> *The Lord is near to all who call on him, to all who call on him in truth.*
>
> **Psalm 145:18**

And whatever you ask in prayer, you will receive, if you have faith.
Matthew 21:22

As the man went away fully healed, he immediately faced opposition. The religious elite was there to condemn a man who had just seen freedom for the first time in thirty-eight years. Jesus warned often that this kind of opposition will certainly face those who choose to believe and follow him.

He forewarned his followers to **stay alert**. Their faith would be attacked. They would be persecuted. Wars and rumors of wars would come. People would come claiming to be the Messiah. False prophets would rise up.

His remedy is not to tell them how to avoid it. He doesn't give them an inside clue on when he will return so that they can be ready. He just tells them to stay alert, to be on guard. He urges them not to be found sleeping on what they have been called to do when he returns.

What does he mean not to fall asleep? Surely we're allowed to rest! What Jesus is warning here is that there are enemies around who are daily seeking to bring harm to the church. People will try to derail us from true faith. However, we must remain vigilant.

We have an incredible mission that Jesus has entrusted the church with before he returns—"*The gospel must first be proclaimed to all nations*" (Mark 13:10). There is Good News that Jesus has overcome death and offers salvation to all who would hear and believe. We have the message, and we have the Holy Spirit guiding us. It is up to us to stay alert and to go!

APPLYING THE WORD

What does it mean to you to stay awake?

What are some dangers or distractions that can pull you away from who God has called you to be and what he has called you to do?

Is there anything that God has put in your heart at some point in your faith that you've never obeyed? Is there a gift or talent he has given you that you know you are not using to bring him glory?

PRAYING THE WORD

In the space below, write out something that especially stood out to you from today's Bible reading. It may be a verse you read, something from the devotion, or just a thought that God gave you. As you close out today's devotion in prayer, pray this back to God as a commitment to him.

DAY 6

The Bread of Life

John 6 - Mark 8

Truly, truly, I say to you, whoever believes has eternal life. ***I am the bread of life****. Your fathers ate the manna in the wilderness, and they died. This is the bread that comes down from heaven, so that one may eat of it and not die. I am the living bread that came down from heaven. If anyone eats of this bread, he will live forever. And the bread that I will give for the life of the world is my flesh.*

John 6:47–51

In John 4, Jesus showed he gives us living water. Here in John 6, he is the **Bread of Life**. A food theme might not be what you wanted to see in the middle of a fast! I pray that you let today's devotion speak directly to your cravings. Let Jesus remind you that more than bread, more than water, he is our greatest need. He is the one who will sustain us for all eternity.

EXAMINING THE WORD

Read John 6

Here in John 6, huge crowds were following Jesus for one reason—he was doing great miracles. In the miraculous feeding, how much bread did Jesus begin with and how much was left over?

Jesus urges the crowd to not look only for physical food but for eternal nourishment. Write out verse 27 in your own words.

Compare verse 34 to John 4:15. Now read verse 35 again. What does this tell you about Jesus?

John 1:14 states, "The Word became flesh." In verses 52–57, he invites his hearers to eat of his flesh and drink his blood. Many of the followers turned away from following after this teaching. What is Jesus saying here? Consider that his flesh represents the Word of God, and his blood represents redemption and eternal life.

Read Mark 8

In feeding this crowd, how much bread did Jesus begin with and how much was left over?

Peter's confession in verse 29 is the turning point in the Gospel of Mark. What did he confess to Jesus? What do you think is the significance of Jesus's disciples beginning to recognize this?

Focus on Jesus's action verbs in verses 34–35, "If anyone would ***come*** after me, let him ***deny*** himself and ***take up*** his cross and ***follow*** me. For whoever would ***save*** his life will ***lose*** it, but whoever ***loses*** his life for my sake and the gospel's will ***save*** it." How do we lose our life for the sake of the Gospel?

REFLECTING ON THE WORD

Our theme for today is Jesus's first of seven "I AM" statements in John. He said, "**I am the Bread of Life**." Bread is one of the oldest prepared foods on the planet, originating some 6,000 years ago. Bread radically changed civilizations from being hunter/gatherers to building more complex societies because for the first time people had a sustainable food source.

The process of making bread is quite fascinating. The basic ingredients of any bread are flour, water, and a touch of salt. That's it! None of these have any significant nutritional value. Attempting to live on these three things alone and you would die within only a few months.

However, when the fermentation process begins through the yeast found naturally in the air, the three simple ingredients of flour, water, and salt undergo a complete transformation. The yeast causes the bread to rise. It breaks it down and releases hidden vitamins and nutrients. When the process is complete and the dough is baked, these three nutritionless elements have now transformed into a superfood that has the power to sustain people and transform societies.

Jesus said he is the Bread of Life. The people in Israel at that time would have known the value of bread. They knew droughts. They knew hunger. Archeologists have found that bread encompassed up to 70% of what the people of Israel ate. As a matter of fact, in Hebrew, the word for bread, *lechem*, is even synonymous with food in general.

In a society where bread is so deeply vital to survival, a part of every meal they ate, Jesus said, "I am your bread." He wants to be that for you. He doesn't say to work for it; he just invites us to take it. He wants to sustain you. He wants to fill your basket. He wants to transform you. And he doesn't need anything else to do it! The ingredients you need to be transformed by Christ were put in you by the one who created you.

So God created man in his own image, in the image of God he created him; male and female he created them.

Genesis 1:27

APPLYING THE WORD

We are six days into the fast. How is your fast going? Is God building a hunger in you for anything new spiritually?

Jesus is the Bread of Life because he is the Word of God. What are some ways you can consume more of God's Word?

When we don't eat physical food, we experience hunger pangs. When we stop feeding ourselves spiritually though, we tend to just stop feeling anything at all. Our soul quietens. How can you know when you are hungry spiritually?

Fasting causes us to deny ourselves as we focus more on God. Jesus ultimately denied his flesh as he prayed, “Not my will, but yours,” and then later carried his cross to lay down his life for us. What does it mean to you to deny yourself and take up your cross? How can you do that today?

PRAYING THE WORD

In the space below, write out something that especially stood out to you from today’s Bible reading. It may be a verse you read, something from the devotion, or just a thought that God gave you. As you close out today’s devotion in prayer, pray this back to God as a commitment to him.

DAY 7

Jesus, the Christ

John 7 - Philippians 2

*On the last day of the feast, the great day, Jesus stood up and cried out, "If anyone thirsts, let him come to me and drink. Whoever believes in me, as the Scripture has said, 'Out of his heart will flow rivers of living water.'" ... When they heard these words, some of the people said, "This really is the Prophet." Others said, "**This is the Christ**."*

John 7:37–38, 40–41

Today is the final day of Week 1! I hope that God has spoken to you and revealed new things to you this first week—things about yourself and things about who he is and who he wants to be in your life. If you've slipped up, maybe skipped a day, don't beat yourself up. You've made it here today, so finish the week out strong. We've seen that Jesus is the Word of God, he is love, and he is the Bread of Life. As we wrap up the first week, we're going to look at him as the Messiah—the Christ—the Anointed One sent to save us.

EXAMINING THE WORD

Read John 7

In verse 7, why did Jesus say "the world" hates him?

Why do you think Jesus ended up not only going into Jerusalem but even publicly teaching at the temple after saying he would not go?

What one work was Jesus referring to in verse 21 that he had done? Look back at John 5.

Write out verse 38. What is the living water that will flow out of those who believe in him?

Read Philippians 2

In verse 2, Paul asks his readers to complete his love by being four things. What are they?

In verses 7–8, although Jesus was God what did he choose to do?

Humbling himself to the point of death, God highly exalted him so that at the name of Jesus, what will happen?

Verse 14 tells us to do all things without grumbling or disputing. In what areas is this hard for you?

REFLECTING ON THE WORD

More important than what Jesus did during his ministry is understanding who he was. Some saw him simply as a miracle worker, some as a prophet, some as a deceiver, even others as simply a carpenter from Galilee.

The theme today is **Jesus, the Christ**. If Jesus was not the Christ, if he was not the Messiah, if he was not God in flesh, then what was it all for? If his sacrificial death did nothing to atone for sin, then Jesus's ministry lacked any eternal significance. If he did not truly overcome the grave and rise from the dead, then he was a failure. He was unable to do what he said he would do.

A title regularly associated with Jesus is Christ. *Christ* is the Greek word for the Hebrew term *Messiah*. It literally means "the Anointed One," from the Hebrew word for anoint (*mashach*). This title carried incredible weight for the Jewish people who had been eagerly awaiting a Messiah for centuries. The Messiah was the one chosen by God to preach the gospel of salvation to the nations and to set the captives free.

You can see then the incredible significance in Jesus telling the people he was the Christ. He was the one they had been praying for. He was the fulfillment of the many prophecies. Look at what Jesus declared to the people below.

> *The Spirit of the Lord is upon me, because he has anointed me to proclaim good news to the poor. He has sent me to proclaim liberty to the captives and recovering of sight to the blind, to set at liberty those who are oppressed, to proclaim the year of the Lord's favor.*
>
> **Luke 4:18–19 (quoting Isaiah 61:1–2)**

Imagine the centuries of Jewish people praying and waiting for their Messiah. Parents passed down the prophecies to their children who eventually passed down to their own children. So many had claimed to be him and weren't, but they never gave up hope.

Why was so much weight placed on this one person? In one word—*salvation*. They were a people with a history filled with enslavement and foreign occupation. Their ancestors had been forced into foreign lands. Even now, they lived under the rulership of the Roman government. The Messiah would bring salvation. The Christ would finally bring true freedom.

That is who Jesus is, but now ask yourself, "Who is he to me?" Is he your salvation? Is he your freedom? Let the reality of who Christ is wash over to you today.

APPLYING THE WORD

Why do you think so many people were unable or unwilling to recognize Jesus as the Christ, the Anointed One? Why are they unwilling today?

In John 7:38, Jesus, referring to the outpouring of the Holy Spirit, said all who believe in him will have rivers of living water flowing from them. What does this mean to you? What would it look like in your life to have the Spirit daily flowing out of you?

In Philippians 2, Paul said to do everything without grumbling or disputing, so that we can shine as lights in this dark and crooked world. Is there something that you have done way more complaining, arguing, or worrying about than trusting God?

Peter declared to Jesus, "You are the Christ." Who is Jesus to you? In a few sentences, answer the same question as if Jesus is asking you directly, "Who do you say that I am?"

PRAYING THE WORD

In the space below, write out something that especially stood out to you from today's Bible reading. It may be a verse you read, something from the devotion, or just a thought that God gave you. As you close out today's devotion in prayer, pray this back to God as a commitment to him.

DAY 8

The Light of the World

John 8 - 1 John 1

This is the message we have heard from him and proclaim to you, that **God is light***, and in him is no darkness at all. If we say we have fellowship with him while we walk in darkness, we lie and do not practice the truth.*

1 John 1:5–6

As you're beginning the second week of your fast, you've probably learned a little bit about your self-will. You may have found it easier than you thought. You may have given up after the first day. Stop for a moment and think about your first week. What were the highs? What were the lows? How did your schedule for reading and prayer work out? Are there any adjustments that need to be made before continuing?

Wherever you're at, remember—this is a process! This process isn't to give us spiritual pride if we accomplish it or spiritual shame when we struggle. It is about deepening your relationship with God. This week should begin to be less about dealing with the shock of changing your daily habits and fighting cravings and more about having the Holy Spirit to start to take you to a deeper level in your walk with Christ. This is what the fast is all about!

EXAMINING THE WORD

Read John 8

In response to the crowds from chapter 7 continuing to question who Jesus was, he boldly declared to them in 8:12 that he is the light of the world. Look back to John 1:3–5. Jesus knew that the darkness would never be able to do what?

If two witnesses were needed to validate a testimony. Who else bears witness about Jesus (8:18)?

Jesus tells his hearers in verses 31–32 that if they abide in his word then they would know the truth, and the truth would set them free. What is the truth Jesus is talking about? Look back at verses 23 and 28–29.

According to verse 47, whoever is of God is able to hear his words. What do you think he means by that?

Read 1 John 1

John here calls Jesus the Word of Life in the first chapter of his letter. He also called him the Word in the first chapter of his Gospel. In verse 3, he says they proclaim him so that there will be fellowship. What does fellowship with God and the church mean to you?

In verse 5, John gives them the central message and reason for writing the letter. What is the message?

What does verse 7 tell us will happen when we walk in the light?

Summarize verses 8–9. Personalize it by beginning with *“If I say I....”*

REFLECTING ON THE WORD

John began his Gospel affirming Jesus as the light of the world. He wrote, “The light shines in the darkness, and the darkness has not overcome it" (John 1:5). He began his first letter to the church in nearly the same way, reminding them that "God is light, and in him is no darkness at all" (1 John 1:5). Here in chapter 8, Jesus gives his second "I AM" statement, declaring, "I am **the Light of the World**."

This is one of the reasons the Gospel of John is called the "spiritual gospel." John's Gospel was written somewhere close to the end of the first century. This would mean that John spent the majority of his life reflecting on what he had seen and heard from Jesus before writing out the Gospel.

John had decades to ponder over Jesus's statement in John 8 about being the light of the world. He meditated over what Jesus would have meant—the essence of light, the reality of darkness, the people of God receiving and reflecting the light of Christ. By the time of his writing, John had developed a deep and rich understanding of Jesus as the light of the world.

The antithesis of light is, of course, darkness. If you have ever been on a tour of a cave, often when the group gets to a deep cavern, they will seat everyone and turn off all the lights. With absolutely no light penetrating the subterranean space, the darkness can almost be felt. It is often disorienting. Then the tour guide will generally light one tiny flame and the group unanimously breathes a sigh of relief as shapes reappear and senses reorient.

You see, darkness has no power over light. It is not a force unto itself, it is simply the absence of a force. A dark space is merely a space that is currently void of the power of light. However, the moment light appears, darkness extinguishes.

Jesus is the light of the world. His light is the presence of God. His light brings hope; it brings love; it brings life. For those who are in Jesus, His light is in them. His light burns away darkness and cleanses us from sin.

If that is the case, then what power does darkness have? Its only victory is when the light chooses not to shine. When we either avoid the dark places or we go but we hide our lights afraid of what others will think, the darkness goes unchecked.

Jesus tells us to let our lights shine! We have the Gospel, the Good News of salvation, burning within us. Don't mask it. Don't run from the darkness. Choose to be a light wherever God places you today—and watch the darkness flee.

APPLYING THE WORD

What does light signify to you? What are some areas you see light in your world?

What does darkness signify to you? Where are areas you see darkness in your world?

Look at 1 John 1:9. Why do you think confession is so important? Allow the Holy Spirit to search your heart for a moment. Have there been areas of your life that you have been either afraid to confess to God or, perhaps, you have confessed but still do not feel that God could truly forgive you for?

What is an area of darkness (perhaps a specific sin, a fear, a broken relationship, a friend or family member away from God) you can let your light shine into this week? Commit to God to be a light in whatever dark place he puts on your heart now.

PRAYING THE WORD

In the space below, write out something that especially stood out to you from today's Bible reading.

It may be a verse you read, something from the devotion, or just a thought that God gave you. As you close out today's devotion in prayer, pray this back to God as a commitment to him.

DAY 9

Spiritual Blindness

John 9 - Genesis 3

So for the second time they called the man who had been blind and said to him, "Give glory to God. We know that this man is a sinner." He answered, "Whether he is a sinner I do not know. One thing I do know, that though ***I was blind, now I see*** *... Jesus said, "For judgment I came into this world, that those who do not see may see, and those who see may become blind."*

John 9:24–25, 39

Before beginning today, stop for a moment and think about what direction your attitude has been moving through the fast. During an extended fast, it's easy to get into survival mode. You don't want to give up, so you just put your head down and ride it out—force your way through it one day at a time. What you forget is that at the same time, you may be miserable to be around!

Jesus knew people's tendencies during a fast. He told them that when they fasted not to look somber like the others. The hypocrites would make sure everyone around them knows they're fasting. Instead, Jesus said to pick your head up, wash your fast, fast in secret, let your Father reward you, not others.

EXAMINING THE WORD

Read John 9

The disciples held a common belief that this man's blindness could only have been the result of someone's sin. What reason did Jesus provide for his blindness? The works of God should be made manifest in him.

It's interesting that this man's sight wasn't damaged at some point in his life. He was born missing certain components to make his eyes function properly. Jesus used two things to restore his sight—saliva from his mouth and dirt from the ground. Read Genesis 2:7. What did God originally use to create man? Dust of the ground and breathed into his nostrils the breath of life

In verse 16, what was the reason some of the Pharisees were convinced Jesus could not have been sent from God? Because He didn't keep not the Sabbath day.

Instead of publicly celebrating their son's healing and telling the Pharisees who had healed him, the parents just told them to ask their son themselves. Without having all the answers, the man gives one of the simplest, most straightforward testimonies of how his life was changed by Jesus. Write out his one-sentence testimony from verse 25 and then in verse 38.

John 9:25 Whether he be a sinner or not I know not. one thing I know that, wheras I was blind, now I See

John 9:38 Lord I believe. And he worshipped Him

Comparing the blind man with the Pharisees, Jesus said in verse 39 that he came so that those who do not see may see, and those who do see may become blind. What does this mean spiritually?

Read Genesis 3

The serpent began with a seed of doubt. What question did he first ask the woman?

When the serpent had Eve doubting God's goodness, then he directly contradicted the word of the Lord. What did he tell her would happen when she ate of the fruit?

Look at the three ways Eve was tempted in Genesis 3:6. Compare this with 1 John 2:16 and see what three ways we are all tempted. Think about areas you are tempted in, which one of these three do they fit in?

Genesis 3:6	1 John 2:16
Good for food	Desires of the flesh
Pleasing to the eyes	Desires of the eyes
Make her wise	Pride of life

REFLECTING ON THE WORD

Today's theme is **spiritual blindness**. You can see in the above passages how God's Word shows the contrast between those who are blind and those with sight—between physical blindness and spiritual blindness.

By the end of the story of the blind beggar, he could see physically, but his eyes were also opened spiritually as he believed in and worshipped Jesus. On the other side were the religious leaders. They could see physically but were shown to be blind to spiritual truths.

Think about the very first man and woman. They were created in perfect fellowship with God. They enjoyed daily community with him as they walked together in the cool of the day. They did not yet have a fleshly sinful nature to battle with.

Genesis 3 states that once they disobeyed the Father and ate of the fruit, their eyes were opened. Opened to what? To shame, to vulnerability, to regret, to disobedience, to sin. As their eyes were opened to death through sin, their sight was closed to intimate communion with God as they hid in shame and were ultimately cast out of the garden.

Look at what Paul tells us that came as a result of this first sin:

> *Therefore, just as sin came into the world through one man, and death through sin, and so death spread to all men because all sinned.*
>
> **Romans 5:12**

In the first man, humanity had its eyes opened to our sin nature and at the same time was blinded to our spiritual nature. Jesus came as a final Adam (1 Corinthians 15:44) to put to death the power of sin over us and to open our eyes to a new life in the spirit.

> *But I say, walk by the Spirit, and you will not gratify the desires of the flesh. For the desires of the flesh are against the Spirit, and the desires of the Spirit are against the flesh, for these are opposed to each other, to keep you from doing the things you want to do.*
>
> **Galatians 5:16–17**

A physical healing like restoring someone's sight is certainly miracle worthy. However, the greater miracle is that the Light of the World has come to break through our darkness. We were not created to walk under a heavy cloud of sin, doubt, shame, and brokenness. He offers us a solution to our condition. His light is love. It is healing. It is restored communion with God.

APPLYING THE WORD

Spiritual blindness is anything in our lives that blocks us from the freedom Jesus has for us. You are nine days into your fast. Has God revealed to you any areas of spiritual blindness or darkness in your life? unforgiveness, anger, ill talk concerned of what people think

What kind of temptations are you struggling with the most in your fast? Are you having any physical withdrawals? Food

The blind man received his sight after obeying Jesus by going to Siloam to wash his eyes. This was not the only time that obedience preceded someone receiving their full healing after being touched by Jesus. Is there something that God has called you to do that you have not yet obeyed?

Jesus didn't come to condemn blindness but to give sight to those who were enslaved to it. We are called to do the same. Think about those who are in darkness, who have never known the love of Jesus. Pray for them. In Day 8, we discussed that we are to be a light in the darkness. How can you be a light today to someone in spiritual blindness?

PRAYING THE WORD

In the space below, write out something that especially stood out to you from today's Bible reading. It may be a verse you read, something from the devotion, or just a thought that God gave you. As you close out today's devotion in prayer, pray this back to God as a commitment to him.

DAY 10

The Good Shepherd

John 10 - Psalm 23

I am the door. If anyone enters by me, he will be saved and will go in and out and find pasture. The thief comes only to steal and kill and destroy. I came that they may have life and have it abundantly. I am ***the good shepherd****. The good shepherd lays down his life for the sheep.*

John 10:9–11

Sheep don't worry about their next meal. They may walk through dark valleys, but the shepherd always leads them to the green pastures. Today we will see how Jesus is **The Good Shepherd**. Know that he will provide for all of your needs. Allow the words of King David to speak to you today—"*The Lord is my shepherd; I shall not want*" (Psalm 23:1). Find your fulfillment in Christ today.

EXAMINING THE WORD

Read John 10 –

Jesus calls himself the good shepherd. What does he also describe himself as in verse 7? What do you think this means?

Jesus says in verse 9 that all who enter through him will be saved. How do we enter the sheepfold through him?

Write out John 10:10. Underline the three things the thief comes to do.

Take a look at verse 18. Who was responsible for taking Jesus's life?

Personalize verse 28 as Jesus speaking directly to you. Begin with "*(Your name), I give you....*"

Read Psalm 23

What are the four things the shepherd does for the sheep in verses 2–3? Think about the needs of the sheep that each of these fulfills.

1. ______________________________
   (need for rest)
2. ______________________________
   (need for replenishment)

3. ______________________________
(need for restoration)

4. ______________________________
(need for holiness)

Does the shepherd keep his sheep from dark valleys or enemies?

Sheep may have their heads anointed for protection against pests or to heal cuts and infections. What happens in the Psalms once his head is anointed with oil?

The English verb often used in the first part of verse 6 is *follow*. However, the Hebrew verb *radaph* is better translated as "pursue." What does it mean to you that the goodness and mercy of God are actively pursuing his children all the days of their lives?

REFLECTING ON THE WORD

Today's theme focuses on Jesus being **the Good Shepherd**. In John 10, Jesus uses the analogy of a shepherd and his sheep. This chapter gives us the third and fourth "I AM" statements in John as he calls himself the door of the sheep and the good shepherd. Let's break down each character in this chapter as we discover what Jesus is saying to us.

- **Sheepfold.** The sheep that belonged to the shepherd were brought into the sheepfold. A *sheepfold* was a large pen to hold the animals, generally with stone walls and briars on top of the walls to deter predators. The sheepfold represents eternal security for the sheep. It separates who is in the flock and who is not—who belongs to the shepherd and who does not. For those who belong to God, there is a place where they can find rest, safety, restoration, and protection from the harsh outside world.
- **Door.** The sheepfold had a single entrance that would be securely shut at night as the shepherd kept watch at the opening for any vandals that would seek to harm or take the sheep. Before calling himself the shepherd, Jesus first calls himself the door.

He is the only entrance to the sheepfold—to eternal life. Jesus will say later in John, "*I am the way, and the truth, and the life. No one comes to the Father except through me*" (14:6).

- **Thief.** The thief wants only to steal the sheep from the sheepfold. Jesus describes robbers who sneak into the body and quietly make off with a single sheep. Then, in verse 12, he describes the thief as a wolf who drags his victim away to devour him and scatter the other fearful sheep.
  The thief is the same thief from the beginning in Genesis 3. He is the Great Deceiver. Satan stands as an adversary to the people of God (1 Peter 5:8). He is powerless against the Shepherd, so he tries to drag one believer away at a time through false teaching, deception, and doubt. He knows that if he can pull away one, he can cause others to doubt as well.
- **Sheep.** Sheep are particularly vulnerable animals. They are for the most part defenseless to robbers and wolves that would come to take them away. Sheep have few natural defensives. They don't have sharp teeth or claws. They don't have tough or thick skin. They aren't even very fast or strong. Their

only two protections from any outside force are the flock and the shepherd.

Sheep are the most mentioned animals in all the Bible. They often represented innocence and purity. Sheep were the most commonly sacrificed animals in the Old Testament. The people of God were often referred to as sheep throughout the Bible.

- **Shepherd.** Shepherds were either hired by wealthy landlords, or as King David, they were the youngest son in the family. Shepherds knew their sheep personally one by one. They led them to food and water daily and then counted them that evening as they brought them back into the sheepfold. They would then guard the sheep at the door through the night to protect them from enemies.

  Jesus uses the same analogy as David did in Psalm 23, calling himself the Good Shepherd. He has an intimate knowledge of his sheep. He knows their cries, and they know his voice. He desperately searches when one is lost. And most importantly, he lays down his life for his sheep.

How Jesus loves us and wants to have a personal relationship with us! Jesus doesn't describe himself as a great ruler over his people. He says it in a way that expresses his humility and desire for an intimate connection—I am the Good Shepherd. In our insatiable desire to be independent in today's culture, we often mock people who choose to be followers by calling them sheep. The truth is, we're all following something (Romans 6:16–18). Jesus never mocked people for being sheep, he just said they need a Shepherd.

APPLYING THE WORD

1 John 4 warns us, just as John 10 and Psalm 23 do, that there are enemies that come to pull people away from the truth. John warns that they will speak from the world and not from God. Jesus says though that his sheep will know his voice. How can you know when the voice you are feeling in your spirit is from God?

The thief comes into the communion between the Shepherd and his sheep in the same way the serpent came into the communion between the Father and Adam and Eve. Think about the three things (steal, kill, and destroy) the thief has tried to do in your own life.

What does he want to **steal** from you? Is it joy, peace, purpose, community?

What does he want to **kill** in your life? Is it hope for the future, dreams, plans, relationships?

What does he want to **destroy** in your life? Is it your integrity, your faith, a career?

PRAYING THE WORD

In the space below, write out something that especially stood out to you from today's Bible reading. It may be a verse you read, something from the devotion, or just a thought that God gave you. As you close out today's devotion in prayer, pray this back to God as a commitment to him.

Goodness and mercy will overtake me. It will pursue me.

DAY 11

Raised to Life

John 11 - 2 Corinthians 5

*Jesus said to her, "**I am the resurrection and the life.** Whoever believes in me, though he die, yet shall he live, and everyone who lives and believes in me shall never die.*

John 11:25–26

You are halfway through your fast! Continue to soak up all that God has for you in this. Find joy in the process. Discover intimacy with God in the journey. You will read today about the raising of Lazarus from the dead. Lazarus may have been raised to life, but he still had to pull off the grave clothes. It's hard to convince others you're walking in new life when all they see is death, gloom, misery, frustration, and despair surrounding you. Today is about walking in the freedom that Christ has given us.

EXAMINING THE WORD

Read John 11

This chapter introduces the siblings Mary, Martha, and Lazarus. The two sisters pleaded with Jesus to come by saying, "*He whom you love is ill.*" They were in Bethany, less than two miles from Jerusalem, but Jesus had already traveled an entire day's journey away from Jerusalem. What had just happened that led him to head east out into the wilderness? Look back at John 10:39.

What reason did Jesus tell his disciples he was glad that he was not there when Lazarus had died?

Focus on verses 25–26. Reflect on what it means to you.

Verse 35 is the shortest English verse in the Bible. Why do you think Jesus wept? Look back at verse 33. What does this tell you about the heart of God when we are hurting?

What were the religious leaders really afraid of in verse 48 that led them to want to kill Jesus?

Read 2 Corinthians 5

Paul compares our limited physical bodies to a tent and our future bodies to a house. He says our desire is not to be found *unclothed*, in other words, becoming bodiless spirits just floating around after death. Look at verse 5. Who has prepared our new bodies and how can we have confidence in that?

What does it mean to you to be controlled by the love of Christ?

Paul explains that Jesus died for us all. So, if we are "in Christ," then we also died to our old selves. When Christ rose again to new life, we also rose to live a new life through him. Knowing that, write out verse 17.

Jesus has reconciled us back to wholeness, back to intimate communion with God. What does it mean to you that we now have the ministry of reconciliation?

REFLECTING ON THE WORD

Today's chapters focused on us being **raised to life** in Christ. It's exciting to think about the resurrection and eternal life that Jesus offers to us. In chapter 11, he gives his fifth of seven "I AM" statements as he declares "*I am the resurrection and the life.*" Having a new life in Christ first requires death to our old lives. Take a look at what Paul says in Romans about dying to our old selves so that we might live with Christ.

> *For if we have been united with him in a death like his, we shall certainly be united with him in a resurrection like his. We know that our old self was crucified with him in order that the body of sin might be brought to nothing, so that we would no longer be enslaved to sin. For one who has died has been set free from sin. Now if we have died with Christ, we believe that we will also live with him.*
>
> **Romans 6:5–8**

Jesus's miraculous resurrection of Lazarus was just an example of what he wants to do for every one of us. He came to reconcile us with the Father, to take us back to that Garden of Eden experience where Adam and Eve had a perfect relationship with God—before sin created a separation.

How can Jesus make this kind of promise? How can we know that if we follow him that a new body and eternal life are waiting for us? In John 11:25, he said, "*I am the resurrection and the life.*" This is how! Jesus didn't just perform a miraculous resurrection; he *is* the resurrection. He didn't just bring a person back to life, he *is* life.

Salvation is not a thing; it isn't an experience; it's not a prayer. Salvation is a person. His name is Jesus. That's why Paul said in 2 Corinthians 5 that "*if anyone is in Christ, he is a new creation.*" If we are in him, we have overcome death because he overcame death. We have eternal life because he is eternal life. And, most importantly, we are made one with the Father because he is one with the Father.

The sad thing for many Christians, though, is that we have been set free, but we still walk around with the mindset of a slave. The prison doors have been flung wide open, but we prefer the security of the four walls and iron bars.

Lazarus had already been raised to life, but he was still wrapped up in his grave clothes. The remnants of his life that had passed, the smell of death, and the bindings that confined his hands and feet still limited him from experiencing his new life. Jesus commanded that these bindings be removed so he could experience what was already a reality. It was time for him to look and walk like a man who was living, not dead.

The resurrected life doesn't just begin at death. It begins the moment we die to ourselves and place our trust in Christ. We begin to live in him, and his Spirit comes to live within us. At that moment, we are eternal beings. Unfortunately, though, temptations, fears, and bad habits can still stick around. This is what maturing in faith is all about—stripping off the grave clothes and learning to walk in the freedom that Jesus has already declared over us.

APPLYING THE WORD

Jesus was moved in compassion to the point of tears over the pain in those he loved and their lack of faith that their brother could be raised again. Do you consider yourself a compassionate person? How do you think you develop this kind of compassion for others?

What do you think it looks like to be spiritually alive in Christ but still walking around in grave clothes, held down by your old life? Does this relate to anything in your life?

We are ministers of reconciliation. This means that God has chosen us to share the love of Jesus with as many people as possible so that they can experience the same new life that we have experienced. Does it intimidate you to share your faith with others? Pray and ask God for boldness this week. Who are some people (maybe just one person) that you can share with about what Jesus has done in your life?

PRAYING THE WORD

In the space below, write out something that especially stood out to you from today's Bible reading. It may be a verse you read, something from the devotion, or just a thought that God gave you. As you close out today's devotion in prayer, pray this back to God as a commitment to him.

DAY 12

Anointed by Jesus

John 12 - 1 Samuel 16

But the Lord said to Samuel, "Do not look on his appearance or on the height of his stature, because I have rejected him. For the Lord sees not as man sees: man looks on the outward appearance, but the Lord looks on the heart ... Then Samuel took the horn of oil and ***anointed*** *him in the midst of his brothers. And the Spirit of the Lord rushed upon David from that day forward. And Samuel rose up and went to Ramah.*

Titus 3:4–7

Today we're digging into the word *anointed*. No matter where you feel like you are on your spiritual journey, where you are with your relationship with God, if you are saved, you are anointed! You have the power of purpose of God resting on you!

EXAMINING THE WORD

Read John 12

Mary, who had just seen Jesus raise her brother back to life, was now watching her once-dead brother Lazarus reclining and eating with the Lord. How did she anoint Jesus?

She anointed Jesus feet with perfume

More than 2,300 verses in the Bible are about money or possessions, far more than prayer, faith, or heaven and hell. It was a common subject of Jesus's teaching as well. He knew the enemy can use the love of money to drag people into pride and away from the heart of God. What does verse 6 say Judas was secretly doing with the group's money? Judas was pilfering the money

Stealing

Again, we see those who were spiritually blind having their eyes opened and those who thought they had sight revealing themselves to be blind. In verses 9–11, what are the two different reactions to Jesus?

Write out verse 25 in your own words. Personalize it by beginning with *"If I love my…."*

Look at the themes of light and darkness again in verse 46. What happens to those who believe in Jesus?

Read 1 Samuel 16

Why was Samuel in mourning at the beginning of the chapter? Take a look at the two passages below for some context.

Then Samuel took a flask of oil and poured it on [Saul's] head and kissed him and said, "Has not the Lord anointed you to be prince over his people Israel? And you shall reign over the people of the Lord and you will save them from the hand of their surrounding enemies. And this shall be the sign to you that the Lord has anointed you to be prince over his heritage.

1 Samuel 10:1

The word of the Lord came to Samuel: "I regret that I have made Saul king, for he has turned back from following me and has not performed my commandments." And Samuel was angry, and he cried to the Lord all night.

1 Samuel 15:10–11

Summarize how the Lord said he looks at people in verse 7. The Lord looks at the heart

NEVER be afraid of the future God has for you

Look at verse 13. What happened to David the moment he was anointed?

REFLECTING ON THE WORD

Here in John 12, we're beginning the final week of Jesus's earthly ministry. On Day 7 we discussed **Jesus, the Christ**. Today, we continue that theme with what it means to be **anointed by Jesus**. To *anoint* someone meant to rub oil on them, generally on their head or forehead. This may seem like a strange practice, but it has had deep significance for the people of God for thousands of years.

The sacred act of anointing sets someone apart. It positions them for a special purpose. As kings, prophets, and priests were chosen, they were then anointed to signify that they now held a position of leadership and authority over God's people. Even more than that, with the anointing also often came the filling of the Spirit.

After David was anointed, where did he go? Straight to the throne? No, right back to the field to keep caring for the sheep! He had an anointing on him, he had the Spirit of the Lord in him, he had the calling, he had the empowerment, but

God still had him in a testing period. He was still being matured, still being prepared for the time that he would walk in the anointing that he had been called to.

He may have gone back to the fields, but he never forgot about the anointing that rested on him. Just because it didn't happen immediately didn't mean he lost faith that it *would* happen. He didn't discount what had happened. He was patient and he walked out the path the Lord had placed him on.

Here's the thing, the anointing of God isn't reserved just for the great leaders of Scripture. If you are a born-again follower of Jesus Christ, you have been anointed by God. You will read tomorrow in 1 John 2:20 that "*you have been anointed by the Holy One.*"

What does it mean that you have been anointed by Christ? It means you've been called by the Most High God for a specific purpose, and you have been empowered by his Spirit to accomplish it. Your anointing is the fuel to your engine. It is the helium in your balloon.

When you choose to trust in God fully and walk in the anointing he has placed over your life, just as the psalmist wrote in Psalm 23:5, your cup will begin to overflow. You will begin to see things of the Spirit that you didn't even know were in you—love, confidence, joy, compassion, hope, boldness—beginning to flow out of you like never before.

APPLYING THE WORD

The comparison is often made between Martha, who worked hard at preparing a meal for Jesus and his followers, and Mary, who sat at his feet in worship. Which one do you relate more to in how you serve Jesus?

If you are saved, you are anointed. You have been called and empowered by God for a purpose. What is something you feel like God has put in your heart that you have been called to be or to do?

What are some things you would like to see begin to overflow in your life? After writing them, boldly make your requests known to God.

PRAYING THE WORD

In the space below, write out something that especially stood out to you from today's Bible reading. It may be a verse you read, something from the devotion, or just a thought that God gave you. As you close out today's devotion in prayer, pray this back to God as a commitment to him.

DAY 13

A New Commandment

John 13 - 1 John 2

A new commandment I give to you, *that you love one another: just as I have loved you, you also are to love one another. By this all people will know that you are my disciples, if you have love for one another."*

John 13:34–35

Fasting can lead us to spiritual breakthroughs, not only for us, but also for our families, churches, and nations. When Nehemiah heard of the complete destruction of Jerusalem, he was shaken to the core. The Bible says that he wept for days and then committed to praying and fasting. His resolve to turn to God, to humble himself before his creator, was the first step in turning the heart of a king and setting into motion a plan that would see the restoration of Jerusalem.

In fasting, we realize that it's not all up to us. We may not have the strength within us. We may lack the answers to the problems that plague us. But we serve a God who is strong enough, who does have the answers. Let this fast humble you. Use this fast to bring your greatest needs before God. Trust that he will move, a breakthrough can happen.

EXAMINING THE WORD

Read John 13

Take a look at Matthew 26:14–16. What had Judas just done before the meal? He made a deal with the chief priests to hand JESUS over to them

In verse 13, Jesus calls himself their Teacher. His method of teaching was to put on the garments of a servant and then bend down to wash their feet in humility. How does he tell them to respond in verse 14? They should was one another's feet.

Write out verse 34. A new command I give you. Love one another. As I haved loved you, so you must love one another.

Look at verse 35. In what way will people know who is a follower of Jesus? If we love one another

Read 1 John 2

Who is our advocate who forgives us and declares us as righteous before the Father? Jesus Christ, the Righteous One

What does it mean to say that we know God but refuse to obey him? He is a liar and the truth is not him.

Write out verse 9 in your own words. Personalize it by beginning with *"If I say I am...."*

In verse 22, how does John describe the antichrists, the deceivers who try to pull people away from the faith?

In verse 25, what promise do those who abide in Jesus have?

REFLECTING ON THE WORD

John introduced us to the love of God in John 3 with Jesus explaining that God's love for us was the very reason he came into this world. His compassion shined as he healed, he forgave, he fed, and he raised the dead to life. Jesus described his extravagant love for us as a shepherd's love for his sheep—that he would stop at nothing to protect them, to seek them when they are lost, and even to lay down his life for them.

Now here in John 13, only hours before his arrest and crucifixion, he issues **a new commandment** to his followers. Now that they have seen the love of God in the flesh, Jesus tells them to now go and love one another with that same kind of sacrificial love.

Loving one another is not an option, it is a commandment. Jesus said, "*A new **commandment** I give to you.*" Loving one another is also not relegated only to those who love us back. Jesus didn't add that we only have to love someone *if* they do this or *unless* they do that. It is mandated for all.

In fact, loving others is the one way Jesus said that the outside world is allowed to judge the authenticity of our faith. In John 13:35, he said by this one thing they're going to know whether or not you're truly one of my followers. Why is this? Because our horizontal love gives evidence to the reality of our vertical love. How can someone have the love of God come fully alive in his or her heart and then continue living in hatred for others?

Although it is a commandment, Jesus did not just command love, he modeled it. Before telling his followers to love one another, he demonstrated it magnificently by washing their feet. Jesus knew Peter would deny him three times. He knew Judas would soon betray him. And yet, Jesus showed real love by bending down in the position of a servant and washing their feet.

Think about how Jesus showed his love. He humbled himself, he served, he obeyed his Father, and he laid down his life. He calls us to do the same. As we do, we reflect the heart of God. To love God is to glorify God. To love others with the love God has given us is to shine his glory in the world.

Love is not an easy task. For Christians, it is the greatest of callings. *Love* is one of those words that sounds attractive until we've been hurt—until we've been let down, abused, neglected, betrayed, or abandoned. That's when we get a glimpse of the kind of love that could compel Jesus to bend down and wash the feet and eat a meal with someone who was just about to turn him over to be arrested and killed.

True sacrificial love does not come naturally to us. We want to repay others with how they treat us. If you're good to me, I'll be good back to you. But, if you mistreat me, you better watch out! The incredible thing about the love of God though is that it has nothing to do with the actions or feelings of the other person. We do not love someone because they are *whatever you have decided makes someone worthy of your love*. We love because God is worthy. Love is our greatest act of obedience to God.

APPLYING THE WORD

What is one thing that has surprised you about yourself during this fast, good or bad?

How do you define *love*?

If you asked people around you, how do you think they would describe you in terms of how you love, serve, and sacrifice yourself for others? Be honest!

Ask God to put in your heart if there is someone that you've hurt or that has hurt you in the past. How about those who are in your life today but for whatever reason you do not get along? What would it look like to humble yourself and love them in the same way Jesus did for his disciples?

*Loving others does not mean subjecting ourselves to unhealthy or abusive environments.

PRAYING THE WORD

In the space below, write out something that especially stood out to you from today's Bible reading. It may be a verse you read, something from the devotion, or just a thought that God gave you. As you close out today's devotion in prayer, pray this back to God as a commitment to him.

1/28/23

DAY 14

The Holy Spirit

John 14 - Galatians 5

But the helper, ***the Holy Spirit****, whom the Father will send in my name, he will teach you all things and bring to your remembrance all that I have said to you. Peace I leave with you; my peace I give to you. Not as the world gives do I give to you. Let not your hearts be troubled, neither let them be afraid.*

John 14:26–27

You are now finishing your second week of the fast. This is a perfect time to think and meditate on the Holy Spirit and consider: What voices do I allow to speak to me? Am I walking by the Spirit or only by what my flesh tells me? As the physical temptations hopefully begin to quieten some as your body is adjusting, now is the time to tune in to the voice of God! Sometimes he shouts to get our attention, but most of the time it's a whisper.

EXAMINING THE WORD

Read John 14

In verses 1 and 27, Jesus tells his disciples to not let their hearts be troubled. Why would they be troubled? Look back at John 13:33.

Jesus says where I am going you cannot come

How does Jesus describe the Father's house? What promise does he make to his followers in verse 3? The Fathers house are many dwelling places

Jesus promises to prepare a place for his followers and receive them and they will be together with Jesus

Think about verse 6.

The **way** to what? Father

What **truth**? Jesus

What kind of **life**? eternal

Write out verse 14. If you ask anything in my name, I will do it

In verse 17, where does Jesus say the Holy Spirit dwells? abides in me and will be in me

In verse 26, think about in whose name the Holy Spirit always comes. What does Jesus say he will teach us? The Holy Spirit comes in Jesus name. The Holy Spirit will teach me all things and bring to Remembrance all that He said to me

Read Galatians 5

In verse 1, Paul says that Christ has set us free. In 2 Corinthians 3:17, he also says, "*The Lord is the Spirit, and where the Spirit of the Lord is, there is freedom.*" In what ways do you think we could end up submitting again to a yoke of slavery?

Read verses 13–15, then summarize them in your own words.

Verse 16 tells us that we will not gratify the desires of the flesh when we walk by the Spirit. Clearly Christians still sin. Why do you think Christians still struggle with this, if they are being led by the Holy Spirit?

Write each fruit of the Spirit. Beside it, put what the opposite would be for those who live by the flesh.

1. Love - Hate
2. -
3. -
4. -

5. Kindness - faction
6. goodness - immoral
7. faithfulness - impurity
8. gentleness - disputes
9. Self control - carousing

REFLECTING ON THE WORD

The theme for today has been weaving through John's Gospel since the beginning. It is **the Holy Spirit**. Here in John 14, Jesus knew he would soon be departing. His betrayer had already left too soon to bring his accusers to arrest him.

Jesus saw the fear, the anxiety, on the faces of his disciples. How did he comfort them? He didn't say everything was going OK, that he would be able to avoid being arrested, that they could avoid persecution. No, Jesus told them that although he would be going soon, he would be sending the Spirit.

With the Spirit, Jesus promises in John 14:12 that his followers could do even greater things than he did! How is that possible? How can the church do even greater works than Jesus who healed, fed thousands, and even raised people from the dead? He knew that as long as he was *with* us, he was God in flesh, but that was God in the flesh of one man—one body. Jesus *in* us, however, is the Spirit of God poured out on the church—the body of Christ.

The Holy Spirit is not a *thing* that Jesus promised his church—it is a *who*. And that *who* is God. The Holy Spirit is the Spirit of God; he is the Spirit of Christ. What does it mean to receive Christ at salvation? It means to receive his Spirit.

The Spirit of God has been there since the beginning. He hovered over the waters in Genesis 1:2. He was there waiting for the Word of God to go forth. When the Word was spoken, the Spirit went out to give life. The Spirit of God (Holy Spirit) will not operate outside of the Word of God (Jesus).

The Spirit was also the breath that poured into the lungs of Adam giving him life. This wasn't just a one-time thing. That is a role of the Spirit. He brings dead things back to life. He breathes life into things that seemed hopeless. Actually, the Hebrew word for breath and spirit are the same—*ruach*.

On the day of Pentecost in Acts 2, just as Jesus promised, his Spirit poured out. The church was born. What was one body was now the living body of Christ. What was the Spirit *with* us became the Spirit *in* us—giving us hope, giving us strength, giving us freedom, and giving us life. If you are a believer, that same Spirit is in you.

APPLYING THE WORD

How wou you describe the Holy Spirit to someone else?

Have you felt the Holy Spirit guiding you or perhaps convicting you at points in your life?

As a Christian, the Holy Spirit dwells in you. He is there to guide, to teach, to defend, and to empower you to do the work of God. Knowing that, how should that change how you live? How should it change how you pray?

Paul describes the fruit of the Spirit in nine ways. Before you pray, write two of these that you need more of from the Holy Spirit. Why did you choose these two?

PRAYING THE WORD

In the space below, write out something that especially stood out to you from today's Bible reading. It may be a verse you read, something from the devotion, or just a thought that God gave you. As you close out today's devotion in prayer, pray this back to God as a commitment to him.

The Holy Spirit will teach me
And bring things to Remembrance

I have anger
lacking in patience
But because of the
Holy Spirit I can walk
in patience, peace, Joy

DAY 15

No Longer of the World

John 15 - 2 Timothy 2

If the world hates you, know that it has hated me before it hated you. If you were of the world, the world would love you as its own; but because you are not of the world, but ***I chose you out of the world****, therefore the world hates you.*

John 15:18–19

Today begins the final week of your fast. If you've been staying faithful, great job. If you slipped up some or maybe gave up completely, don't worry! Just jump back in again for this last week. Today's theme is a great kick-off for your final seven days. For people in the world, choosing to deny yourself for three weeks may not make sense. Skipping meals or shutting down social media to read and pray may seem foolish to them.

Jesus encourages us though that he has chosen us. He warns us that not only will many in the world not understand our faith, but that the world will hate us. However, there is also good news. We were chosen for a purpose. We have an opportunity to bear witness to the love and hope of Jesus.

EXAMINING THE WORD

Read John 15

Pruning cuts out any parts of the branch that are dying or diseased. It may seem counterproductive to cut something down so that it can grow stronger, but ultimately it builds the branches up and allows it to grow fruit. How does this process of the Father pruning away what is unhealthy to allow the branch to grow more fruit compare to us spiritually?

In verse 8, how do we glorify God?

Look at verse 9, how much does Jesus love us?

In verse 19, what reason does the world hate us? What does that mean to you? In what ways do you think believers are hated by the world?

Read 2 Timothy 2

Reading verse 1, what gives us strength?

In verses 3–6, Paul gives three examples to describe a faithful and dedicated follower of Jesus.

What are they? Which one connects with you the most?

In verse 14, he warns the church not to just argue over words. Is there an example of that you have seen in the church?

Paul goes on to tell him to avoid irreverent *babble* (worthless, foolish talk) in verse 16. In what direction does this kind of empty talking lead people?

Summarize and then pray verses 22–23 as a personal commitment to God. Begin with "*I will flee....*"

REFLECTING ON THE WORD

Each of the chapters today discussed what it means for a follower of Jesus to be **no longer of**

the world. Jesus told his disciples that they were still *in* the world, they just weren't *of* the world any longer. What exactly does that mean? Look at what Paul told the Philippian church.

> *But our citizenship is in heaven, and from it we await a Savior, the Lord Jesus Christ, who will transform our lowly body to be like his glorious body, by the power that enables him even to subject all things to himself.*
> **Philippians 3:20–21**

Gaining citizenship to another country can be a long and oftentimes challenging process. Depending on the country, there are many different rules and processes to follow even if a person qualifies to become a citizen.

What many have found after gaining citizenship in the new country they have moved to is that they have lost their citizenship from the country they were born in—generally, to never be regained again. Should they go back home to visit, they are now visiting as outsiders. The soil they were born on is now foreign soil under their feet. Their visit may be for a week or even a year, but it is temporary. It has an expiration.

Jesus will say later in John 18:36 that his "*kingdom is not of this world.*" He is telling his followers that their citizenship has been transferred. Dual citizenship is not an option! If they have been born again, if they have been transformed by Christ, then they are now citizens of heaven. They have a new and glorious homeland that is now awaiting them.

With this incredible promise of a new, eternal home and a new, glorified body also comes a grave warning. Jesus warned his disciples that the world would now hate them as it hated him. The world would now persecute them as it did him. They would be rejected by those who used to call them brothers, treated as outsiders by their own people.

This warning carries no less weight today. Too many Christians have fooled themselves into thinking dual citizenship for their soul is possible, as if they can serve Christ and the destructive desires of this world. Read Jesus's words during the Sermon on the Mount.

> *No one can serve two masters, for either he will hate the one and love the other, or he will be devoted to the one and despise the other. You cannot serve God and money.*
>
> **Matthew 6:24**

Jesus declared his final "I AM" statement in this chapter, "*I am the true vine.*" Pursuing Christ is not about what we lose but what we gain. We become attached to Christ, like a branch grafted to a vine. We have a new source of life flowing into our veins.

Discover the joy of being *in* this world but not *of* it. Discover the freedom of fleeing the things of this world—brokenness, rebellion, selfishness, pride, division, destructive desires. Through Christ, we have been transformed. Whether you feel it or not, you have the power to overcome sin through the Spirit inside of you. Remember, stand strong and walk in the confidence of your calling. You are a citizen of heaven.

APPLYING THE WORD

Write down something that you have learned about yourself over these past two weeks.

Jesus said he is the vine and we are the branches. He tells us to abide in his love. What does that mean to you?

Have there been times that you have felt like an outsider because of your faith?

Jesus so often warned against focusing too much on money or success. Why do you think it's such a big deal to the Christian faith?

Have you ever felt a conflict between your walk with God and your desires for personal success?

PRAYING THE WORD

In the space below, write out something that especially stood out to you from today's Bible reading. It may be a verse you read, something from the devotion, or just a thought that God gave you. As you close out today's devotion in prayer, pray this back to God as a commitment to him.

DAY 16

Mourning into Joy

John 16 - Psalm 40

Truly, truly, I say to you, you will weep and lament, but the world will rejoice. You will be sorrowful, but ***your sorrow will turn into joy*** *... So also you have sorrow now, but I will see you again, and your hearts will rejoice, and no one will take your joy from you. In that day you will ask nothing of me. Truly, truly, I say to you, whatever you ask of the Father in my name, he will give it to you. Until now you have asked nothing in my name. Ask, and you will receive, that your joy may be full.*

John 16:20, 22–24

We all know the story of Jonah and the big fish. After trying to run from God, Jonah finally went to Nineveh and preached the message of the Lord to this wicked nation. When they realized how wrong they had been and that they needed to repent, what did they do? They fasted. Every man, woman, child, and even animal in the nation humbled themselves before God. They prayed and fasted in repentance.

Fasting moves the heart of God because it moves our hearts. It releases the grip that our flesh so often has on us and allows our spirits to begin to shine through. With our hearts and minds clear, we can begin to see things as they really are.

EXAMINING THE WORD

Read John 16

In verse 1, Jesus tells his disciples, "*I have said all these things.*" Take a glance back at chapters 13–15 to see what things he is talking about. What one teaching of Jesus from the past three chapters stands out to you the most?

Jesus told them in verse 2 that they would be put out of their synagogues. That meant they would be rejected from the religious and social structure that they have been a part of their entire lives. What reason does he tell them they will be killed?

Verses 13–15 are some of the most revealing words of Jesus concerning the Holy Spirit. Summarize what he says about the role of the Spirit.

Jesus describes his death and resurrection as a woman giving birth, with sorrow and then with joy. Remember Jesus's words to Nicodemus in John 3:3, "*Unless one is born again, he cannot see the kingdom of God.*" Explain how believers in Jesus Christ also go from sorrow to joy when they are born again.

Read Psalm 40

King David wrote this psalm during a time of great distress. He compares hopelessness, depression, and despair to what kind of ground?

He compares the steadfast love of God to what kind of ground?

In verse 3, David said he will have a new song to sing because God lifted him out of the darkness he was in. But even more than that, what does David say will happen with others because they see what God has done for him?

Stop and pray the entire Psalms back to God. Think about some dark areas you've walked through or that you're walking through now. Personalize the prayer by beginning with, *"God, I waited patiently for you to help me, and you..."* When you've finished, write the one sentence that speaks to you the most.

REFLECTING ON THE WORD

The theme for today is **mourning into joy**. Don't miss the keyword "into!" It is not "mourning *or* joy," "joy *instead of* mourning," or "joy *in spite of* mourning." Jesus makes it clear that his followers will experience joy—inexpressible, incomprehensible, eternal joy.

However, just as the sheep of Psalm 23 found their great feast and green pastures *through* the dark valley, our pathway to joy must also come *through* the reality of pain and suffering. Look at what the Apostle Paul writes to the church of Philippi to prepare them for the suffering they would be going through.

> *For it has been granted to you that for the sake of Christ you should not only believe in him but also suffer for his sake.*
>
> **Philippians 1:29**

For any of us who have lived this life long enough, we surely don't have to be convinced that suffering is a reality of life. It is often said that if you are not right in the middle of a storm, you're either heading into one or out of one. Suffering presents itself in innumerable ways—death of loved ones, disease, health issues, mental issues, job loss, divorce, rejection, loneliness—the list goes on and on.

Jesus knew he wouldn't have to convince his followers that they would face hard times. In the passage in John today, he is preparing them for the time when he would no longer be with them. They knew problems would keep coming, but they were so used to having Jesus right there by their side.

When they couldn't feed a crowd or quiet a storm, Jesus was there. When they failed to catch any fish or cast out a demon, Jesus was there. But very soon, he wouldn't be there, at least not in the way they wanted him to be. He would send his Spirit, but they would have to learn to recognize him and to trust in the Spirit within them as much as they trusted in Jesus in front of them.

Throughout the Bible, whether the suffering was from bad choices or persecution, the response of God was the same. His faithfulness never wavered. His forgiveness never reached its limit. Our God never stops pursuing his people! In each chapter, God made the same promise: he would turn their sorrow into joy.

Weeping may tarry for the night, but
joy comes with the morning.
Psalm 30:5b

God's promises still ring true today. Consider the trials you have faced and the sorrow you have endured. You may be the person who wears it like a protective suit around you. Because of what you've experienced in the past, you're not going to let anything hurt you like that again. You keep your hopes at a minimum and people at a distance. Or, you may be the person who buries it deep down within you. You know how to laugh, to smile, to socialize like everyone else, but there is hurt within you that others aren't allowed to see. You keep it there because you haven't figured out how to deal with it. You think you're holding it in, but the truth is, it's holding you down.

God's Word said that our mourning, our sorrow, can be transformed *into* joy. He knows what we've been through. He knows our past. He knows our fears. He wants to take all of it and use it for joy.

How is that possible? It's possible when we recognize that there is eternal hope beyond the temporary pain. There is light on the other side of the darkness. God can use even the darkest parts of our stories and turn them into testimonies of his faithfulness to see us through.

And, how do we get to the joy? We ask. It's not a secret. The journey may be long and hard at times, but the promise of joy is there for those who believe. Jesus said, "*Ask, and you will receive, that your joy may be full.*"

APPLYING THE WORD

Put yourself in the disciples' shoes that night. Less than a week ago they walked into Jerusalem to a massive crowd celebrating Jesus. Now, one of their closest friends has just betrayed their Lord. Jesus is telling them his life will be taken shortly and they will surely be hated by the world and face incredible persecution. What emotions would you feel?

In what areas of your life do you see joy?

We all face suffering in different ways—mourning, sorrow, grief, distress, anguish, pain. Sometimes it is because of our faith in Christ and sometimes just because of not following his direction. What are some areas in your life you have faced suffering that still affect you today?

What would it look like to see joy come through that? You may not have an answer to that right now. If not, just stop and pray for God to begin the process of healing and revealing to you how to move to a place of joy. Don't be afraid to ask for it in Jesus's name.

PRAYING THE WORD

In the space below, write out something that especially stood out to you from today's Bible reading. It may be a verse you read, something from the devotion, or just a thought that God gave you. As you close out today's devotion in prayer, pray this back to God as a commitment to him.

DAY 17

Perfectly One

John 17 - 1 Corinthians 12

Holy Father, keep them in your name, which you have given me, that ***they may be one****, even as we are one ... The glory that you have given me I have given to them, that they may be one even as we are one, I in them and you in me, that* ***they may become perfectly one****, so that the world may know that you sent me and loved them even as you loved me.*

John 17:11, 22

You only have five days remaining in this fast. You may be close to the end, but don't focus on the end, focus on the journey. Today's theme is **perfectly one**. God wants nothing more than to have a closer relationship with you. He wants to walk with you daily just as he did with Adam and Eve. Allow the last several days of this journey to draw you into God's heart like never before. Experience what it means to walk in oneness with God.

EXAMINING THE WORD

Read John 17

In verse 1, what posture did Jesus take when he began to pray? What does that speak to you about his relationship with the Father? His posture was looking toward heaven

Close, trust

We often think of eternal life as a place we go to after death. How does Jesus define eternal life in verse 3?

Eternal life: that we know only true God, and Jesus Christ, whom God sent

Jesus asked the Father to "*glorify your Son that the Son may glorify you.*" Jesus then says in verses 10 and 22 that he would be glorified in us. How would you define *glory*, and what does it mean to you that Jesus is glorified in us?

Glory-magnificence, great beauty

Honor, high Renown

In verse 17, how are we *sanctified* (purified or made holy)? We are Sanctified by the truth. The Word of God

Verse 26 shows that if we are one with God, the same eternal love that the Father has for the Son is the love he has for us. What does it mean to you to know that God loves you that much?

God will never let me down
Loves me knowing all my faults
Loves me for me

Read 1 Corinthians 12

Paul tells the church that before they came to Christ, there was ignorance (verse 1), deception (verse 2), and blasphemy (verse 3). What is the only way someone can truly proclaim that Jesus is Lord? by the Holy Spirit.

In verses 4–6, he explains that we may have different gifts and callings in the church, but what is the main point he is stressing? Same God at WORK in everyone and all of the different gifts.

List each of the nine gifts mentioned here in verses 8–11. (You can compare to the seven gifts Paul lists in Romans 12:6–8)

Write out verse 26. Personalize it by replacing "one member" with "I." After writing, consider what it tells us about how the church was created to interact.

REFLECTING ON THE WORD

Jesus's prayer in John 17 is often called the "High Priestly Prayer." It magnificently shows the heart of Christ for us as he prayed to the Father only moments before he would be betrayed. What was the focus of this final prayer before heading to the garden? What did he choose to ask of the Father on behalf of his followers?

Jesus prayed for unity. He prayed in John 17:23 that we would all become "**perfectly one.**" Our oneness is vital to the world knowing that we are his, and it is something that, sadly, the church has struggled with and more often failed at since its inception.

The problem with the unbelieving world is not the message of the Gospel, it is the messengers for the Gospel. A broken, disunified, divisive church can hardly effectively show the world a God of unity.

We do not worship three gods, but one Holy God who has three expressions —Father, Son, and Spirit. God is in perfect unity with himself. Remember the words of Jesus to Philip in John 14:9, "*Whoever has seen me has seen the Father*."

The church is the body of Christ. Paul did not say in 1 Corinthians 12:27 that we are *like* the body of Christ. He said we *are* the body of Christ. We are no longer individuals trying to figure out life on our own. We are each a single member of a greater body.

We lose that in our individualistic culture today. Our faith often becomes what we get out of our spiritual experiences. The problem with having that mindset is that we do not identify ourselves as the church. Instead, the church becomes something separate from us. We say things like, "I go to that church. I missed church last Sunday. I'll watch church online." What does that mean? It means, "I'm not the church, the church is something separate from me."

That's not what the church is called to be. Paul explains that we are one body but just like a body, there are many different parts. Each part serves a different purpose. Imagine the foot refusing to be connected to the leg or saying, "I'll do my job as long as I get something out of it." We know that the body isn't there to serve the foot. The foot exists to serve the body.

Have there been times in your life that you've felt like something is missing in your life? The truth is, that void may not be there because you need something else in you, it may be that you need to be a part of something greater than you.

A church without unity is as dysfunctional as a body without unity. In a body, health issues will be rampant. In a church, members will continuously lack fulfillment. Growth will be stunted. We need to understand the oneness that we have been called to.

When we as a church begin to walk in unity, the Holy Spirit is manifested in the body. When favoritism and division are replaced with love and harmony, the gifts of the Spirit begin to flow from the head, which is Christ. We can walk in the power of Christ when we walk in unity as the body of Christ.

APPLYING THE WORD

Where have you seen favoritism in the church?

Spiritual gifts are not skills or talents. They are special gifts given by the Holy Spirit to members of the church to build up the body. Looking at the list Paul gave in 1 Corinthians 12 and Romans 12, do any of these speak to you that you might have a passion for or that you have seen come out of you when serving others?

Is there an area in your heart that lacks unity? Perhaps you've been scarred by a negative church experience or by another believer. Perhaps you're continuing to hold a grudge against someone because of something they've done. Jesus knew these issues would come but still calls us to be one. What is something you can do to restore unity in that situation?

Would you say that at times you are overly critical of the church? Do you quickly judge others and their decisions, but take offense when others judge you back? If so, how can you begin to be a person who champions unity in your church?

PRAYING THE WORD

In the space below, write out something that especially stood out to you from today's Bible reading. It may be a verse you read, something from the devotion, or just a thought that God gave you. As you close out today's devotion in prayer, pray this back to God as a commitment to him.

The problem with the unbelieving world is not the message of the gospel it is the messengers for the gospel

DAY 18

Treasure in Jars of Clay

John 18 - 2 Corinthians 4

But ***we have this treasure in jars of clay****, to show that the surpassing power belongs to God and not to us. We are afflicted in every way, but not crushed; perplexed, but not driven to despair; persecuted, but not forsaken; struck down, but not destroyed; always carrying in the body the death of Jesus, so that the life of Jesus may also be manifested in our bodies.*

2 Corinthians 4:7–10

This fast has most likely tested you—physically, mentally, emotionally, and spiritually. As this fast nears its end, don't lose sight of what God is doing within you through the process. James says that "*the testing of your faith produces steadfastness*" (James 1:3). It's hard to see how much endurance has been built up within you until you learn to look back and appreciate where he has brought you. It's like the person training for a marathon who each day runs a little farther. After months and months of training, they are finally able to go 26.2 miles. Ask yourself today, "What has this test taught me? Where do I see endurance being built up?"

EXAMINING THE WORD

Read John 18

Jesus and his eleven disciples would have walked a little over a mile from the upper room, across the Kidron Valley, and up to the Garden of Gethsemane. Judas knew he would find Jesus and the other disciples there. He did not come alone though. Who all came with him to confront and arrest Jesus?

John recorded the seven "I AM" statements of Jesus. Here in the garden, the moment Jesus declared "*I am he*," everyone around him fell to the ground. John doesn't give more detail, but why do you think his declaration caused the crowd to fall back?

Peter had just attempted to kill the high priest's servant. Right after that, verse 15 tells us he then snuck into the high priest's courtyard. Why do you think he would go there and risk being crucified as well?

After standing before Annas and Caiaphas, they then led Jesus to Pilate's headquarters hoping to get approval to have him executed. In verse 33, what was Pilate's first question to Jesus?

In verse 38, Pilate asks Jesus, "What is truth?" Look back at John 14:6. Where is the answer he is looking for?

Read 2 Corinthians 4

In verse 4, Paul says the god of this world has blinded unbelievers from the truth of the Gospel. What does this mean to you?

If Satan has blinded those who do not believe, what light has the ability to make them see again?

In verse 7, what does the treasure in jars of clay show to the world?

In verses 8–9, Paul shows the reality of suffering for Christians, but then also of the hope beyond suffering. Write out each comparison.

Afflicted in every way	but not	crushed
	but not	
	but not	
	but not	

Write out 2 Corinthians 4:16 in your own words. Personalize it by beginning with "*I will not....*"

REFLECTING ON THE WORD

The theme for today's reading is **treasure in jars of clay.** My prayer for you is that this fast has begun to reveal to you even more (or perhaps for the first time) that you have an incredible treasure within you. You are more than just flesh and bone.

Paul uses this analogy of jars of clay in 2 Corinthians 4 to encourage the persecuted church. As he shared about the light of the Gospel that shines out into the darkness, he then tells them that they have this light within them.

In ancient times, clay vessels were quite common. Archaeological digs around historic biblical regions often uncover heaps of clay shards from broken pots. Clay jars were the cheapest and most commonly used storage vessels. They would usually be used to hold water, food, grain, or other personal items. Some, though, have been found buried with valuables in them. The problem was that they were also easily damaged or broken.

Paul's point was *not* to remind the church that they're getting old, that their bodies will eventually break down like a bunch of old clay pots! He was reminding them to not lose heart. What they were facing, what they could see on the outside, was temporary.

Our outer jars of clay are not meant to carry on forever. For Christians, the treasure within us is far more valuable than the vessel on the outside. It may be hard to see it at times, but his glory lives within us and can shine out of us as a beacon of hope to others.

In John 18 and Luke 22, we read about Jesus's arrest. The interrogations have begun. The mob is growing. Soon Jesus's earthly body would be broken, and he would breathe his final breath. Yet in all that, he did not waiver. He boldly declared that he had a kingdom not of this world, that they would see him seated at the right hand of the power of God. He knew that the betrayal, the suffering, the beating, the humiliation, the rejection, all of it was temporary.

Peter, on the other hand, wasn't there yet. He showed incredible loyalty in trying to fight off the entire band of Roman soldiers—even though all he managed to do was slice off the high servant's ear! He showed great bravery in sneaking into the home of that same high priest to watch over Jesus and even refusing to leave after being identified by the servant girl. However, what he thought he was doing for the good—lying to keep from getting caught and killed for attempted murder—was instead focusing on temporary self-preservation and not the eternal implications of denying his Lord.

Know today that whatever trials you face—they are temporary! The rejection or betrayal you have faced—it is not eternal! You have a treasure within you. That treasure is the light of the Gospel. Don't spend your life absorbed only with protecting and preserving the jar of clay on the outside. Instead, discover the light within you and let Christ shine through you!

APPLYING THE WORD

You are nearing the end of your 21-day fast! Only a couple more days to go! Share something that God has been revealing to you.

Think about what was going through Peter's mind that night—battling between denying for self-preservation and probably facing crucifixion. Where do you think you'd be? How do you respond now when you have an opportunity to stand for Christ?

In the four comparisons Paul gives in 2 Corinthians 4:8–9, which one speaks to you the most? Why?

PRAYING THE WORD

In the space below, write out something that especially stood out to you from today's Bible reading. It may be a verse you read, something from the devotion, or just a thought that God gave you. As you close out today's devotion in prayer, pray this back to God as a commitment to him.

DAY 19

Living Sacrifice

John 19 - Romans 12

I appeal to you therefore, brothers by the mercies of God, to ***present your bodies as a living sacrifice****, holy and acceptable to God, which is your spiritual worship. Do not be conformed to this world, but be transformed by the renewal of your mind, that by testing you may discern what is the will of God, what is good and acceptable and perfect.*

Romans 12:1–2

Only two days away from completing your fast, now is the time to start preparing for a new challenge—"How do I go forward?" The tendency at the end of an extended fast is to splurge on anything and everything that we couldn't during the fast! If you're fasting from some kind of food, you've probably already planned out everything you want to eat as soon as this is over.

After a few days of it, we forget how far God had brought us. We forget the joys of spending time with him daily. We forget the freedom of having control over our flesh. So, in a few days, enjoy your steak or whatever that special thing is for you. But in the process, don't forget. Take time today to reflect on where he's brought you and how you can carry it forward after the fast concludes.

EXAMINING THE WORD

Read John 19

What was Pilate's verdict on Jesus that he shares in verses 4 and 6? Why do you think he still gave in to demands for Jesus to be crucified?

Pilate's verdict on Jesus is not guilty.

Pilate gave in to the demand because he didn't want to oppose Caesar and wanted to keep his status (selfish)

Pontius Pilate had been placed as the Roman prefect in Judea with the role to keep the peace between the Jewish people and their Roman occupiers. Any failure to control mobs or a lack of loyalty to Caesar would have certainly resulted in losing his position and possibly even physical punishment. What did the chief priests say to Pilate in verse 15 in a way to force his hand?

We have no king but Caesar

Verse 30 is "ground zero" to the Christian faith. It is the moment Jesus gave his life as a sacrifice so that we could become the righteousness of God. Think about Jesus's last words before breathing his final breath. What do they mean to you?

Jesus work for me was complete on the cross

Who reappears in the Gospel in verse 39 that years earlier had gone to Jesus in the night to question him? Nicodemus

Read Romans 12

Paul urges the church to present their bodies as a "living sacrifice." What does that mean to you?

To live according to God's will His Word. In obedience.

going without....

Write out Romans 12:2. And do not be conformed to this world but be transformed by the renewing of your mind so that you may prove what the will of God is that which is good and acceptable and perfect

List each of the seven gifts mentioned here in verses 6–8.

Prophecy
Service
teaching
exhortation
giving
leadership
mercy

In verses 9–21, Paul lists out the twenty-three marks of a true Christian. These are not issues of salvation. We are saved by faith alone. These are qualities that should naturally flow out of us *if* we have truly been transformed and have the Holy Spirit living within us. Of the twenty-three, choose the five that speak to you the most.

Love
Do not be haughty in mind
Do not take Revenge
Overcome evil with good
Be at peace with all men

REFLECTING ON THE WORD

Sacrifice involves giving up or away something. Sacrifice costs. In biblical times, the cost was often a life. For centuries rams, lambs, goats, and doves were slaughtered in sacrifice to God. These deaths were a stark symbol of the devastating result of sin.

Imagine being a Jewish person heading up the rocky path to Jerusalem with your family for the Passover. You are one among a sea of pilgrims converging on the city with your sacrifice in tow. The streets of Jerusalem resound with cheering, singing, dancing, commerce, and, of course, the sound of thousands of lambs prepared for slaughter.

The scene would have been unimaginable. In that same city, with the same throngs of people, with the same thousands of unblemished lambs prepared for sacrifice, would have stood Jesus before the religious leaders. The connection was not lost on his followers. Jesus was the perfect Lamb of God prepared to pay the ultimate sacrifice to redeem humanity.

Sacrifice often makes us think of death, but in Romans 12:1, Paul tells us to present our bodies as a **living sacrifice**. How are we able to do that? How are we able to present ourselves—in all our flaws, imperfections, bad habits, and brokenness—before a perfect and holy God as an acceptable sacrifice? Pay close attention to what he says. It is only *"by the mercies of God."*

Mercy triumphs over judgment.
James 2:13

If God has given us so much, forgiven us of so much, how do we respond? We respond to his sacrifice by presenting ourselves back to him as a living sacrifice. We died to sin through his death and now live in freedom through his resurrection.

Paul then says that *this* is our spiritual worship—not singing, not dancing, not clapping—this act of giving everything I am to God in complete vulnerability and authenticity is how I worship him.

Despite what you think of yourself, you were created by God in his very image. You are of infinite value to him. There is no greater gift you can give than to offer your life back to him. Stop conforming to what's around you. Stop trying to live up to the empty expectations. Let your life be a sacrifice to him and allow him to transform you daily through his love.

APPLYING THE WORD

What do you think of when you hear the word *sacrifice*?

Reading today all that Jesus endured before his death in John 19, how do you think we should respond as Christians to his sacrifice?

From Romans 12:2, what does it mean to you to be transformed by the renewal of your mind?

Of the five marks of a true Christian you chose above, write them out as a prayer to God. For example, "God, let my love always be genuine. Help me never stop holding fast to what is good...."

PRAYING THE WORD

In the space below, write out something that especially stood out to you from today's Bible reading. It may be a verse you read, something from the devotion, or just a thought that God gave you. As you close out today's devotion in prayer, pray this back to God as a commitment to him.

DAY 20

All Things New

John 20 - Revelation 21

And he who was seated on the throne said, "Behold, I am making ***all things new****." Also he said, "Write this down, for these words are trustworthy and true." And he said to me, "It is done! I am the Alpha and the Omega, the beginning and the end. To the thirsty I will give from the spring of the water of life without payment.*

Revelation 21:5–6

Today's theme is **all things new**. The Christian life is not about learning to be better and do better. The purpose of this fast was not for our Christian merit badge so that others can be impressed at how spiritual we are. Jesus did not say do better. He did not say impress me with your good works. In fact, what he actually invites us to do is to die—die to our old selves, our old desires, our old attitudes, our old patterns of sin. Then, he tells us to come live a real life in him. Paul wrote, "*If anyone is in Christ, he is a new creation. The old has passed away; behold, the new has come*" (2 Corinthians 5:17).

EXAMINING THE WORD

Read John 20

John records Mary Magdalene arriving at the tomb early that Sunday morning. From Mark 16:1, notice who else went with her. Mary, mother of James and Salome

John, the author of this Gospel, was the first to arrive back at the tomb. He describes the face cloth as neatly folded and placed to the side. Why do you think he includes that detail?

In his first words spoken following his resurrection, what two questions did Jesus ask Mary in verse 15? What does each of these questions tell us about Jesus's heart for her?

Why are you weeping?
Whom are you seeking?
He cares for Mary.

Jesus's first words to his disciples following the resurrection were "Peace be with you." What does this also tell you about his desire for his followers? Compare that to what they were feeling in the same verse.

Scripture doesn't say that Thomas touched Jesus's side and his hands. Jesus said Thomas believed because he saw him. Thomas made two declarations of who he knew Jesus to be in verse 28. What were they?

Read Revelation 21

Here in the next to last chapter of the Bible, John receives a vision of the new heaven and new earth. Heaven is not about a place but a perfect, restored relationship between man and God. Think about the perfect communion with God as you read verses 3–4. Write out verse 4 as a prayer directly to God. Begin with *"God, you will wipe...."*

In verse 6, what does God give to the thirsty?

life without Cost

In ancient Israel, inside the temple was the holy of holies—a perfect cube-shaped room that housed the ark of the covenant and the very presence of God. Only the high priests could enter (and only once a year at that). Here, the entire city is described as a cube. All of heaven is like the holy of holies. According to verse 22, why is there no need for a temple in heaven? The Lord God, the almighty and the Lamb are its temple

Why is there also no need for a sun or moon in heaven? The glory of God has illumined it and its lamp is the Lamb.

REFLECTING ON THE WORD

By 2007, Gabriela had all but given up hope on life. With severe heart failure and a recent string of heart attacks, the reports from her cardiologist were to prepare for the worst. With her failing health, Gabriela had gone from living to surviving, and then from surviving to simply waiting to die.

As if given a priceless gift from above, Gabriela unexpectedly happened to be approved for heart surgery in the fall of 2007. The doctors were amazed when she woke up with no pain, no complications, and no concerning numbers.

This loving wife, mother, and grandmother wasn't just given an organ, she was given a new chance at life—a new chance to love, to be loved, to laugh, to cry, to prepare a meal for her family, to tell her grandkids about the good old days.

The theme for today is **all things new**. Imagine if Jesus had not resurrected from the dead. If the Gospel of John ended in chapter 19, with Jesus's death and burial, then what we are left with is sacrifice without hope—forgiveness without freedom. Where is the freedom in us having the chains of sin removed and the prison doors of condemnation flung wide open if we haven't even been empowered to walk out?

If Jesus didn't rise to new life, then neither did his church. If that's the case, our faith is solely based on a past event. We can remember the cross, but we cannot hope for the future. Sure, we can rejoice in Jesus's incredible sacrifice, but where there is no new life, we have no confidence in an eternity awaiting us. Paul said in 1 Corinthians

15:14 that if Jesus did not rise from the dead, then everything—the message, our faith—is all in vain!

But Christ *did* rise from the dead! We *do* have hope! For those of us who are in Christ, there *is* new life! Our story does not end in death. It is life through death, freedom through sacrifice. Look at Paul's words in Romans.

> *We were buried therefore with [Christ] by baptism into death, in order that, just as Christ was raised from the dead by the glory of the Father, we too might walk in newness of life. For if we have been united with him in a death like his, we shall certainly be united with him in a resurrection like his.*
>
> **Romans 6:1–5**

The amazing news is that if you are a believer in Christ, your new life does not begin when you leave this world. Your new life began the moment you decided to die to sin and to give your life over to Christ. Our baptism represents a death to ourselves and new birth in Christ—fully united with Jesus.

That means that you have new life in you! You may not see it sometimes; you may not feel it sometimes. But a child does not belong to their father only when they feel like they do. They fully belong to the father at birth. If you are a child of God, regardless of what you think you are or whose you think you are—you are his.

When you gave your life to Jesus, he may have torn the shackles off of you, but you've been too afraid to walk away from the chains. Fear and condemnation can leave people in mental and emotional bondage all their lives. Jesus didn't only come to save us in the afterlife, he came to save every part of us. He wants to see you fully free and walking in new life emotionally, mentally, physically, and spiritually!

> *I have been crucified with Christ. It is no longer I who live, but Christ who lives in me. And the life I now live in the flesh I live by faith in the Son of God, who loved me and gave himself for me.*
>
> **Galatians 2:20**

APPLYING THE WORD

What is the most beautiful or breathtaking place you've ever been to? Thinking about how John describes heaven in Revelation 21, what do you think heaven will be like? Nothing evil NO wrongs, NO hurt, PAIN, NO Struggles

It will be glorious!

Jesus told Mary Magdalene not to cling to him because he had not yet ascended. We cannot physically touch Jesus today, but we can feel his presence and have an intimate relationship with him. How can you cling to Jesus? Prayer, Worship And reading and obedience to His Word.

Think about your life before Christ and since you have been a believer. What has changed? The Bible says that in Christ we are new creations. Do you feel like you are walking in newness of life?

I feel like I'm starting over again to walk in newness of life

If there is something from your old life that Jesus has freed you from, but you are still holding on to, write it here. When Jesus overcame sin and death, he gave us the power to overcome it as well through him. Pray in confidence that God will help you overcome this as well.

God help overcome my past, guilt that I may continue to walk in the new you have for me.

PRAYING THE WORD

In the space below, write out something that especially stood out to you from today's Bible reading. It may be a verse you read, something from the devotion, or just a thought that God gave you. As you close out today's devotion in prayer, pray this back to God as a commitment to him.

DAY 21

Go

John 21 - Matthew 28

And Jesus came and said to them, "All authority in heaven and on earth has been given to me. ***Go therefore and make disciples*** *of all nations, baptizing them in the name of the Father and of the Son and of the Holy Spirit, teaching them to observe all that I have commanded you. And behold, I am with you always, to the end of the age."*

Matthew 28:18–20

Today concludes your 21-day journey of prayer, fasting, and studying God's Word. The theme of this devotional was simply one word—**satisfied**. In Matthew 5:6, Jesus makes a promise: "*Blessed are those who hunger and thirst for righteousness, for they shall be satisfied.*" As you prepare to go forward, remember that it is Christ who truly satisfies.

This world is filled with things that will temporarily satiate our hungers and quench our thirsts. Most of these will only leave us hungry again and quickly searching out more things to fill the void. This is the cycle that Jesus wants to break. Hopefully, this fast has begun to do that in you. Today's theme is **go**. As you go, remember the source, remember the bread of life, remember the well that contains living water. Continue to find your satisfaction in him.

EXAMINING THE WORD

Read John 21

Peter led the way in deciding to go fishing. As the net filled with fish, Peter simply jumped out to swim to Jesus. Look at when Peter was first called by Jesus in Luke 5:4–8. What happened then? Peter fell at Jesus knees and said go away from me Lord I am a sinful man

Jesus could have used his last moments with his disciples to teach them more or to correct them for their lack of faith, but instead, he chose to just have a meal with them. What does this show you about the heart of Jesus?

He loves company/fellowship Spending time with his disciples

Jesus asked Peter if he loved him three times. He first asked Peter if he loved him "*more than these*," meaning the other disciples. Peter had proven to be a strong leader to the others. He even took charge that morning to make sure they had something to eat. But he had also denied his Lord only days before. Why do you think Jesus began with that question?

What exactly does Jesus mean by "*Feed my sheep?*" Think of how Jesus entered into communion and fed his disciples the bread and wine at the Last Supper.

John sums up his Gospel with an amazing closing thought. What does it tell you about all of the teachings and miracles that Jesus actually did throughout his ministry compared to those we read about in the four Gospels?

Read Matthew 28

The religious leaders quickly spread the rumor that the disciples had stolen Jesus's body. Why do you think they would do that?

To discount Jesus Ressurection

Thinking about the details of the resurrection (massive stone, Roman guards, the disciples in hiding, the hordes of people in Jerusalem for the Passover), what makes the stolen body rumor not plausible?

In verse 18, what does it mean to you that Jesus has "*all authority*"?

Matthew 28:19–20 is generally called the Great Commission. Write out Jesus's final command to his disciples before ascending into heaven. Underline the verbs.

REFLECTING ON THE WORD

Today's theme, and the final theme for this book, is simply **go**. As we have seen the heart of Christ through the entire Gospel of John, we know that God's love for us is not based on performance. His satisfaction is not founded in our morality. Salvation does not come from works. However, we also see that an authentic experience with Jesus compels people to action.

The disciples in John 1 were compelled to leave their families, possessions, and livelihoods to follow Jesus. The woman at the well in John 4 was compelled to go and tell the townspeople. The blind man in John 9 was compelled to testify of who healed him.

And then there is Peter. He was always the outspoken leader of the group. He had told Jesus he would die for him, but then days later ended up denying him in the high priest's courtyard.

Here in John 21, Peter led the disciples to return to fishing. John doesn't tell us why they were fishing, but what we do know is that the moment the nets began to fill with fish, Peter knew it was Jesus on the seashore. He was compelled to action. Peter couldn't even wait to put his outer garments back on. He couldn't wait to help the others haul the catch in. He dove in the water to reach Jesus as fast as possible.

Any thoughts of shame for denying his Lord began to wash away in the presence of Jesus. Why? Because Jesus condemned him? Because Jesus rebuked him for having so little faith? Because Jesus reminded Peter that he wasn't even there by his side as the nails were being driven into his hands and his feet?

No, Jesus didn't want condemnation; he wanted community. He didn't want rejection, he wanted a relationship. He chose to restore Peter through love. He asked Peter three times if he loved him and gave him a simple command—*"Feed my sheep."*

The extravagant love of Jesus compelled Peter to **go**. Only weeks later, we see him in Acts 2 boldly preaching to thousands. The Holy Spirit descended. The church was born. Thousands were saved. A movement began that continues until today. It did not begin with rules, religion, or punishment. It began in love.

> *There is no fear in love, but perfect love casts out fear. For fear has to do with punishment, and whoever fears has not been perfected in love.*
>
> **1 John 4:18**

As you wrap up this study, let the love of Christ compel you to **go**. Love calls us to action. In his final words before ascending to the Father, Jesus again told his disciples to **go**. Go and do what? Make more disciples! There is a world filled with people who are beat-up, broken, discouraged, lost, angry, and enslaved. The answer to the hurting and hopeless is not more empty religion. The answer is in a person. His name is Jesus.

Go in love. Go in power. Go in freedom. And as you go, know that he is with you—always, to the end of the age!

APPLYING THE WORD

The goal in this study was to learn that through fasting and pressing into the heart of God, we can learn to be satisfied from above. How has God satisfied you through this journey?

Our relationship with Christ compels us to action. In what ways have you felt led to respond to the love of Jesus?

You see so many in the Gospels who couldn't help but tell others about their encounter with

Jesus. They didn't have all the answers, but they knew what they saw and experienced. If you have been saved, you have a story!

This is your testimony. Have you ever told your story to others who aren't believers? Do you feel intimidated to tell your story?

What is something that you know God has done in your life in the past? How has he blessed you? Where do you see him working now?

Thinking about your family, career, friends, neighbors, and other aspects of your life, how can you respond to Jesus's call to **go**?

PRAYING THE WORD

In the space below, write out something that especially stood out to you from today's Bible reading. It may be a verse you read, something from the devotion, or just a thought that God gave you.

As you close out today's devotion in prayer, pray this back to God as a commitment to him.

CONCLUSION

Thank you for taking part in this 21-day journey. I truly hope and pray that God has used it to speak to you, to give you encouragement, and to ignite within you an insatiable flame to continue to pursue him going forward.

I want to encourage you to take some time to reflect on some of the things that God has shown you about his nature and yourself during this process. Are there people he told you to reach out to, to love better, to forgive? Are there unhealthy habits that you know you don't need to pick back up? Are there healthy habits you picked up during this fast that you know you need to continue? As you reflect, use the space below to write these things out so that you don't forget. Use them to propel into new and deeper places in your relationship with God.

God bless you. May the love of Christ continue to carry you and your family in his incredible grace and through the power of the Holy Spirit.

ABOUT THE AUTHOR

Jeffrey Kent is the administrative pastor at Christ Church in West Monroe, LA, a growing, multisite church in Northeast Louisiana. He is passionate about the local church and has been teaching, preaching, and serving churches for over twenty years including nearly three years on the mission field in China. Prior to accepting the call to move into full-time pastoral ministry, Jeffrey also worked in corporate leadership with experience in mortgage banking and telecommunications.

Jeffrey received a B.A. in Religion from Louisiana College where he received numerous awards and recognitions including the Holman's Excellence in Biblical Studies Award. He also graduated *summa cum laude* from Liberty University with an M.Div. in Discipleship and Church Ministry.

Jeffrey and his wife, Abigail, both live in West Monroe, LA, where they are raising their two children. They love spending time with their kids and investing in their small group community.